D1129305

THE
LOW-CALORIE
Cookbook

THE
LOW-CALORIE
Cookbook

Healthy, Satisfying Meals with
500 CALORIES OR LESS

MEGAN OLSON
Creator of Skinny Fitalicious

PAGE STREET
PUBLISHING CO.

Copyright © 2020 Megan Olson

First published in 2020 by

Page Street Publishing Co.

27 Congress Street, Suite 105

Salem, MA 01970

www.pagestreetpublishing.com

All rights reserved. No part of this book may be reproduced or used, in any form or by any means, electronic or mechanical, without prior permission in writing from the publisher.

Distributed by Macmillan, sales in Canada by The Canadian Manda Group.

24 23 22 21 20   1 2 3 4 5

ISBN-13: 978-1-64567-044-5

ISBN-10: 1-64567-044-9

Library of Congress Control Number: 2019951604

Cover and book design by Meg Baskis for Page Street Publishing Co.

Photography by Megan Olson

Printed and bound in the United States

Page Street Publishing protects our planet by donating to nonprofits like The Trustees, which focuses on local land conservation.

TO MY PARENTS AND MATT,

thank you for always supporting my dreams.

TO MY READERS,

you inspire me daily! Thank you for your dedication.
It means the world to me.

CONTENTS

INTRODUCTION

For as long as I could remember, I struggled with my weight. I dabbled in different diets over the years to lose it, but I could never stay consistent with anything long enough to see real results. I would either restrict my food so much that I would succumb to cravings, or I wouldn't balance my meals properly with carbs, fat and protein, leaving me feeling unsatisfied.

When I was a teenager, my father had a heart attack and my family was advised to eat a high-carbohydrate diet and to cut out fat. I grew up eating fat-free foods and large amounts of processed carbohydrates. I didn't know it then, but eating fat-free foods and highly processed carbs was a recipe for weight gain. These foods are known to have added sugar and chemicals, which increase cravings, and not eating enough fat often leaves us still feeling hungry.

Fast-forward to 2009: I was 210 pounds (95 kg) and at an emotionally difficult time in my life. I was in my midthirties and working as a consultant, traveling weekly, enduring long hours and under immense stress. I didn't enjoy my profession. I felt lonely and abandoned by my friends, who now had families. And I hated my body. I had very little self-esteem and felt unworthy of love (or anything good, for that matter).

Then, one night I took a ten-minute walk on Redondo Beach, California—and those ten minutes changed my entire life.

As I walked on the beach that night, I realized my weight caused me to miss out on so many opportunities in life: not going out with friends and not putting myself out there because I was embarrassed by my weight; hiding at home in my yoga pants with a pizza or a bag of chips; trying to fill the emotional void with food, only to be left with an even deeper void after the food was gone.

That night on the beach, I realized how mentally good that ten-minute walk made me feel, so I committed to walking every night. Months later, I was walking an hour or more and feeling great. It was during those walks though that I realized I had no idea how to eat. After all, there aren't nutrition classes in school that teach us at a young age the proper way of eating and balancing meals. It's sad, really. The most fundamental part of human life is eating, yet we're not taught how to do it the right way.

When I say "the right way," I mean we are constantly surrounded by diet mentality and social media messages that preach to us about eating so-called healthy processed foods (i.e., fat-free foods) or cutting out entire food groups (i.e., keto diets) to lose weight. The reality is these diets and "weight-loss" foods are no better than eating real cake or cookies. A cake is a cake whether it's called Keto, fat-free, low-carb and so on.

Learning to cook and eat real food is something we've gotten away from in our culture. Instead we're buying prepared foods with unnatural ingredients like added sugar, artificial flavors and other chemicals. We're not eating enough vegetables, protein and whole grains—foods that are wholesome and fresh and that leave a person feeling satisfied rather than deprived. These are fundamental foods for losing weight and keeping it off forever.

In 2009, I began teaching myself about food by tracking what I ate using an app called Lose It!. The first time I tracked what I ate, I was astounded by how much I was overeating. I was eating way too many calories and my portions were out of control. For example, prior to tracking I did not realize that a serving of peanut butter is 2 tablespoons (22 g) or that a serving of cooked rice is ½ cup (80 g). Tracking helped me pay closer attention to my portion sizes.

I started measuring my portions and learning to balance my meals with carbs, protein and fat to make them more filling. I also experimented in the kitchen, making my own recipes from versions I'd found on the internet or in magazines. Cooking and creating recipes soon became a passion of mine, and that passion led me to almost effortlessly lose 80 pounds (36 kg) within a year.

After I lost weight, many people kept asking for my weight-loss tips and recipes. So in 2014, I started Skinny Fitalicious, my low-calorie (and gluten-free) food blog. Through my website and social media, I was able to connect with other women who were struggling to lose weight and battling health problems, specifically autoimmunity.

That was when I was diagnosed with Hashimoto's disease. For over a year, I battled severe exhaustion, bloating, GI discomfort and unexplained weight loss. I saw multiple specialists and spent thousands of dollars. It wasn't until I saw a naturopath that I got my diagnosis and began the process of healing by transitioning to a gluten-free diet.

So many women were asking me for help, women who were struggling with weight loss and healing their bodies but didn't know how. It was then that I knew my calling was to help other women. So I left my corporate career, went back to school and became a certified nutrition practitioner. Now I help women over thirty-five lose 20 to 50 pounds (9 to 23 kg) or more—and keep it off.

Never in my wildest dreams could I have imagined that one ten-minute walk would lead me to lose 80 pounds (36 kg), start a website, change my career and generate an opportunity for me to write a cookbook. To have the ability to help other people enjoy healthy eating and lose weight is a gift I will forever be grateful for. I hope this book will not only inspire you to enjoy good food but to reach for what may seem impossible in life.

My food philosophy is that nutrition and weight loss are not about the number of calories you consume. While this is a low-calorie cookbook, many people focus fiercely on the calorie numbers, restricting their diet. This leads to obsessive behaviors with food and vicious cycles of dieting.

A healthy diet is neither a restrictive one based on calories nor one that's a license to overeat and overindulge. A healthy diet is one that's balanced. If weight loss is your goal, your first priority is to eat healthy.

The number of calories in a recipe do not matter unless it has two things: high-quality ingredients and balanced nutrition. By high-quality ingredients, I'm referring to real foods. Not foods made from chemicals that have been created in a lab, have fillers, contain natural flavors and colors not present in a food's original form or contain added sugars. Just because a food has zero calories doesn't mean it's healthy and nutritious. While you may be tempted to replace things like real maple syrup with a zero-calorie syrup, I recommend that you do not.

A calorie is just a number, and that number can be made up of French fries and pizza or nutritious, wholesome, energizing foods. The ingredients that make up that calorie number are really important to your overall health, cravings and energy balance. In general, a healthy recipe is one that is high in protein and high in fiber (from vegetables and complex carbohydrates) with a moderate amount of healthy fat.

As an example, I commonly see people restricting carbohydrates, as they do not understand the role different carbohydrates play in weight loss and a healthy diet. They come to me confused about why they can't lose weight. Their calories are perfect, yet the scale isn't moving. We start adding the right balance of nutrition to their plate—including the right carbohydrates—and suddenly, things are working.

In this low-calorie cookbook, you will see my food philosophy. All the recipes are made with real-food ingredients that are nutritionally balanced. The recipes are meant to boost your energy and make you feel your best. I hope they make you see how delicious calorie-conscious meals can be!

HOW TO LOSE WEIGHT

The healthiest approach to weight loss begins with a major shift in mindset. This means you must stop dieting and start creating a lifestyle with some flexibility.

Most people approach weight loss with an all-or-nothing mindset. They overhaul their food and lifestyle choices in one week and usually give up. That much change is simply too much at one time, and it leads to mental burnout. When they don't succeed or they have a bad day, they feel like a failure and go back to old habits.

The key to lasting weight loss is consistency, because consistency leads to long-term lifestyle change. This means making slow and gradual changes that you can sustain without burning out. But it also means shifting your mindset from feeling like a failure at every setback.

Losing weight requires building new skills, and that is a learning process. Every bump in the road isn't a failure—rather, it's an opportunity to learn and grow. I can show you the perfect way of eating, but if your mindset isn't strong you will always give up at every obstacle.

Mindset is the foundation of lasting weight loss and is something I coach my clients heavily on in my weight-loss programs. Think of your mindset as the foundation of your home. If your foundation is weak, your house will fall down during the very first storm. That strong foundation stabilizes the house so it can weather any storm.

Mindset is key to losing weight and keeping it off for good. When you have the right mindset, implementing good nutrition is easier.

NUTRITION BASICS

Eating for weight loss means getting back to nutrition basics. Many of my clients have been dieting for so long they forget the basics of a healthy diet.

In Chapter 2 (page 21), I will go into more detail regarding nutrition. Good nutrition does not require you to count calories or track macros (protein, fat and carbs). Instead, it's a strategy for healthy eating that will promote lasting weight loss without making you feel overwhelmed.

This is the framework I teach my nutrition clients:

- Eat 6 to 8 servings of nonstarchy produce daily. Starchy vegetables include peas, plantains, corn and potatoes. Anything else I consider a nonstarchy vegetable.

- Incorporate 25 to 40 grams of high-fiber foods every day.

- Incorporate a palmful of lean protein with every meal and snack.

- Eat healthy fats in moderation.

- Cut added sugar. Almost all packaged products contain some form of added sugar. They're even hidden in healthy-looking foods, such as broths, soups, chips, crackers, supplements, flavored yogurts, granola bars, protein bars, oatmeal packs and nut butters, to name a few. Read food labels and look for added-sugar ingredients. Anything that says "sugar," "syrup," "malt" or ends in "-ose" (indicating added sugar) should be avoided.

- Avoid artificial sugars. Artificial sugars are shown to cause gastrointestinal problems such as bloating and diarrhea. They are also known to increase cravings for sugary foods. Stevia and monk fruit are the only two sweeteners I recommend to my clients.

- Eat real sugar—such as maple syrup, honey and coconut sugar—in moderation. These sugars have trace minerals in them. Real food is always a better option over an artificial sugar with zero calories that's made with chemicals. It's unclear what those chemicals do to the body in the long term.

- Avoid processed foods and fast foods.

- Eat three meals a day and limit snacking.

If you choose to track your calories, you'll learn how to do that in this book. Before we get to those details, we need to discuss factors about calories, macronutrients and hormones.

CALORIES ARE IMPORTANT BUT . . .

While this is a low-calorie cookbook, you must understand that weight loss is not as simple as "calories in, calories out." You need a slight calorie deficit to lose weight. The word "slight" is an important distinction here, because science has demonstrated that the human body becomes very efficient with the number of calories it gets during weight loss by lowering the resting metabolic rate (RMR).

An RMR is the number of calories used in basic body functions, such as respiration, circulation, brain function and other tasks that keep you alive, even if you were lying in bed all day.

The mistake most dieters make is creating too big a deficit with their calories too fast and eating below their RMR. When a large deficit is created and you're eating below your RMR, your body enters starvation mode and works to conserve the calories you've consumed by lowering your resting metabolism.

For example, let's say someone has an RMR of 1,500 and goes on a 1,200-calorie diet. Since they're eating below their body's basic 1,500-calorie needs, the body will think it's starving and lower the RMR to 1,200. This is why people plateau with their weight loss or can't keep weight off when they go into maintenance.

Not eating enough calories also leads to hormonal changes in the body, such as, but not limited to, lower active thyroid conversion, an increase in the hunger hormones leptin and ghrelin, an increase in the fat-storing hormone insulin and a decrease in testosterone. These are all things you don't want to happen when you're trying to lose weight.

I've coached women who were consuming 1,200 calories or fewer and eating healthy food, but they were confused as to why they were gaining weight. The body is smarter than we are. It will always attempt to adapt as a survival mechanism, which is why we need to be smart about how we lose weight. Even though we may be eating healthy foods, weight gain can and does happen when our hormones are unbalanced and we're not consuming enough food.

Eating slightly fewer calories (100 to 200 fewer) each week is what I recommend. It may take you longer to lose weight, but it will protect your metabolism and hormones and help you avoid hunger cravings. Always work with a professional to calculate your specific RMR needs. I do not recommend using apps to calculate them, as I've found apps always fall below RMR.

A smaller deficit is also easier to manage because the change is less drastic; therefore, you won't feel deprived and hungry. If losing weight and keeping it off for good is your goal, you shouldn't be in a rush. It must be a lifestyle change.

I can't overstress the importance of eating enough calories, and in my experience working with clients, they're never eating enough calories or the right balance of food, which leads me to my next point.

NOT ALL CALORIES ARE CREATED EQUAL

Remember I said earlier that weight loss isn't as simple as "calories in, calories out." Most people who start following a new diet focus fiercely on the calorie number. The truth is, the number is meaningless unless the macronutrients (protein, fat and carbohydrates) are balanced. This balance is important for keeping blood sugar regulated and hunger levels controlled. This is key to stay consistent with what you eat.

WHY CALORIES ARE NOT CREATED EQUAL

400 CALORIE CHOCOLATE DONUT

400 CALORIE SALMON AVOCADO SALAD

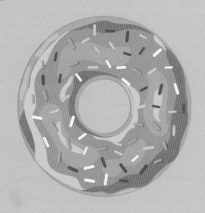

VS

PROTEIN	4		PROTEIN	26
FAT	23		FAT	25
CARBS	44		CARBS	24
SUGAR	20		SUGAR	2
FIBER	2		FIBER	5

When your meals are well-balanced with protein, fat and carbohydrates, you'll feel full and satisfied and have fewer cravings. Those who restrict certain food groups (such as fat and carbs) have more cravings, and cravings are your body's way of telling you that you're missing something in your diet. You may not be getting enough food, you may be getting too much added sugar or you may not be eating enough of the right food in the right balance.

The previous example shows a 400-calorie donut compared to a 400-calorie salmon avocado salad. Each has the same number of calories, but the nutritional profile is very different. The donut has very little protein and fiber yet is high in fat, carbs and sugar. Whereas the salad has a good balance of protein, fat and carbs, very little sugar and a higher amount of fiber.

This means if you eat the donut, you won't feel full for long due to the low protein content and lack of fiber. You'll likely end up craving more sugar shortly after eating the donut. However, if you eat the salad, your blood sugar will remain stable, you'll feel full and you won't feel the need to reach for sugar.

This is why it's important to have the right balance of all three food groups within your daily calorie range. A general daily guideline is 40 percent carbohydrates, 30 percent fat and 30 percent protein. You can use a food-tracking app like MyFitnessPal or Lose It! to track these as a percentage of your daily calories.

Weight loss is more than a number. The type of food you eat impacts hormones, hunger, fullness and cravings. You will always be able to eat far more protein and produce for far fewer calories and feel fuller than if you ate the same number of calories in fat, processed foods and artificial sugars.

While the recipes in this cookbook are lower in calories, the macronutrients are nutritionally balanced for you. This way, you can easily incorporate them into your lifestyle.

FAT-LOSS HORMONES

I've previously mentioned a few hormones impacting weight loss. In this section, I'll talk more about them and their role in weight loss and cravings.

Insulin is the most important hormone. It keeps blood sugar balanced and is also a fat-storing hormone. For instance, when you eat something high in sugar, like a donut, insulin's job is to find a home for the sugar in that donut. There are two places that sugar can be stored: in your muscles or (a tiny amount) in your liver.

If there is no space in those places, your body will generally convert that sugar and store it as fat. This process is no different whether you're eating a donut or a banana. While a banana has more nutrients, the process of finding storage for the energy of the banana is the same as a donut. It's important to note the body has limited space to store energy from sugar, but it has an unlimited space for storing fat.

Another important hormone is leptin. Leptin plays an important role in the body's response to weight loss. Fat cells produce leptin, which inhibits hunger. When you lose weight, levels of leptin in the bloodstream drop, making you more likely to feel hungry. Most people who are overweight are leptin resistant, which means they no longer respond to the hormone and consequently feel hungry more often.

The third hormone, ghrelin, is produced and stored in the stomach and tells your brain when you are full so you'll stop eating. When you're overweight, this hormone is suppressed and does not communicate with the brain, which means you keep eating. It's a vicious cycle when ghrelin or any of these hormones are out of balance.

I'm sure you're now wondering how to balance these hormones. The first step to balancing insulin, leptin and ghrelin is cutting out high-sugar foods, processed foods and added sugars. The second step is eating higher-protein, higher-vegetable meals and snacks with a good balance of complex carbohydrates rich in fiber. This combination will keep your blood sugar balanced so you're not constantly hungry. Consistently eating this way over time, along with getting quality sleep and managing stress, will help balance these hormones.

These hormones are greatly influenced by lifestyle habits, particularly sleep and stress. When you're sleep deprived, your body has less energy and will crave high-sugar foods. When you're stressed or when you overexercise, your body will signal cortisol levels to increase, which will cause you to crave more food. So it's important to address your lifestyle as much as food.

This was a high-level overview of insulin, leptin and ghrelin, and there's much more to them, but what is important for you to understand is that weight loss is more than following a low-calorie diet. Keeping these three hormones balanced is a critical component of losing weight and requires both lifestyle and nutrition interventions.

CUSTOMIZING YOUR CALORIES

Calories, as well as other nutritional information, will be provided with the recipes in this book. Meals will be 500 calories or fewer, and desserts and snacks will be fewer than 350 calories per serving. Remember, fewer calories are not always better. You want to eat above your RMR to lose weight but less than your total daily expenditure. Total daily expenditure includes calories from exercise and daily activities.

To calculate your RMR, use the Mifflin–St. Jeor Equation:

Female: 9.99 x weight (kg) + 6.25 x height (cm) – 4.92 x age – 161 = calories/day

Male: 9.99 x weight (kg) + 6.25 x height (cm) – 4.92 x age + 5 = calories/day

To calculate total daily expenditure:

RMR x 1.2 + calories burned in exercise

Calories may need to be modified depending on if you're breastfeeding, extremely athletic, taller than average, have been chronically under-eating or have specific health conditions. I always recommend working with a nutrition professional when it comes to nutrition and weight loss. Nutrition is often oversimplified, but it is, in fact, a complex field—many factors influence weight loss and nutrition.

HOW TO EAT TO LOSE WEIGHT

In Chapter 1 (page 13), I outlined nutrition basics for balancing meals for low-calorie eating and weight loss. This section covers food groups in more detail, so you can choose foods that give you more energy and cause fewer cravings.

Produce has vital nutrients, and most people are deficient in them, which leads to low energy or cravings. Nonstarchy produce is high in vitamins, minerals and phytochemicals and has disease-fighting antioxidants. These vegetables are high in fiber and water, keeping you fuller longer, and they are naturally low in calories. Nonstarchy produce includes but is not limited to the following:

· asparagus	· cauliflower	· onions
· bean sprouts	· celery	· spinach
· beets	· cucumbers	· squash
· bell peppers	· eggplant	· sweet peppers
· broccoli	· green beans	· turnips
· Brussels sprouts	· leafy greens	· zucchini
· cabbage	· mushrooms	

Starchy produce and grains have higher levels of fiber. These foods are more calorie-dense; however, fiber is shown to increase satiety and promote weight loss. The portion size and quality of these foods matter. Choosing the least processed form is recommended. Examples of starchy produce and grains include the following:

· barley	· legumes	· quinoa
· brown rice	· lentils	· sweet potatoes *& white potatoes*
· corn	· oats	· white rice
· couscous	· peas	· whole fruit
· farro	· plantains	· whole wheat

Carrot,
pumpkin

Protein is a key component in balancing meals. Protein is responsible for balancing blood sugar, building lean muscle tissue and stimulating metabolism. Good sources of protein include the following:

chicken	Greek yogurt	shellfish
cottage cheese	jerky	tofu
egg whites	lean beef	turkey
fish	lean pork	turkey bacon

Fat is essential to healthy hormones and metabolism. Every cell in your body is made with fat, and your brain is 60 percent fat. Good sources of fat include these:

- avocado
- egg yolks
- olives
- raw nuts and seeds (including peanuts and no-sugar-added nut butters)
- unrefined cold-pressed avocado oil, coconut oil and extra-virgin olive oil

HOW MUCH TO EAT

Your overall calorie needs are unique to you, and even if you're not tracking calories and are focusing only on portions, these guidelines will set you up for success when you're choosing what to eat:

- **Protein:** One palm-size portion, or 4 to 6 ounces (113 to 170 g), which equals 20 to 30 grams of protein. Men should get two portions per meal. Women should get one.

- **Fat:** Aim for 1 to 2 tablespoons per meal. Fat is calorie-dense, so it's important to watch the portion size.

- **Starches and grains:** About ½ cup per meal is appropriate. Like fat, starches and grains are more calorie-dense, so watch the portion size of these as well.

- **Nonstarchy veggies and grains:** Aim for 6 to 8 servings daily. You will never overeat nonstarchy vegetables, as they have very few calories—don't get caught up in overanalyzing the portion sizes.

- **Fiber:** When it comes to fiber, 25 to 40 grams (women and men, respectively) should come from your starches, grains and nonstarchy veggies. Don't obsess over the numbers or worry about net carbs (i.e., total carbs minus fiber). Just focus on reaching the fiber number. The goal is to build balanced habits.

Planning is key to creating consistent, healthy eating habits to lose weight. Planning what you will eat in advance saves time, money and calories. Not only that, it reduces the stress around what to eat and yields fewer opportunities to give in to old habits.

I recommend creating a meal plan on the weekend for the week ahead so you can shop, prep and store your meals. This way, you know exactly what you will eat each day of the week and won't be stuck staring at the refrigerator with decision fatigue after a long day of work. This is when unhealthy eating habits happen: when you don't have a plan!

Use the nutrition basics outlined in Chapter 1 (page 13) to build your meals. Protein, nonstarchy vegetables, complex carbohydrates and fat should be planned for in each meal, and in that order.

Meal planning does take practice. I recommend that my clients create one or two meal plans when they're starting out so they can rotate them each week until they feel comfortable creating more. Remember, the more you practice something, the easier it will get as you become more proficient. It's like learning a new sport. Not everyone is an expert on their first try. It takes practice!

HOW TO MAKE A MEAL PLAN

Create a low-calorie meal plan using the following steps:

1. Select the recipes. When selecting recipes for meals, ensure they are under 500 calories; contain healthy, unprocessed ingredients; are high in protein, high in fiber and rich in nonstarchy vegetables. Plan 1 to 2 treats in your week so you don't feel deprived.

2. Plan what recipes you will eat on each day of the week.

3. Schedule when you will make them and prep the ingredients. Scheduling is critical—if it's planned on your calendar, you're more likely to do it.

4. List the ingredients you will need to make the recipes.

5. Inventory your kitchen and cross off ingredients you already have.

6. Shop for your ingredients.

7. Prep the food and store it appropriately.

Stocking your kitchen with key foods and ingredients will prepare you for busy days when you don't have time to make a meal, so you can make something quick and healthy. This habit will set you up for long-term success with low-calorie eating and losing weight. Here are the key foods and ingredients I recommend, organized by storage method (remember to always check labels to avoid added sugar in your foods):

- **Pantry:** Spices and herbs, quinoa, lentils, legumes, brown rice, oats, potatoes, sweet potatoes, extra-virgin olive oil, coconut oil, avocado oil, avocado oil spray, extra-virgin olive oil spray, nut butters, jerky, collagen, maple syrup, honey, coconut sugar, tomato sauce, diced tomatoes, chicken or vegetable broth, almond flour, coconut flour

- **Refrigerator:** Grass-fed butter, ghee, cottage cheese, Greek yogurt, eggs, turkey bacon, milk, vegetables and fruits, unsweetened applesauce, coconut aminos or soy sauce, vinegars, mustards, low-sugar ketchup, hot sauce, salsa

- **Freezer:** Frozen or steamable vegetables, frozen fruit, edamame, potatoes, fish, shellfish, chicken, turkey, lean pork or grass-fed beef cuts, turkey burgers, chicken burgers, lean grass-fed beef burgers, raw nuts and seeds

CRAVINGS

Because this is a low-calorie cookbook for weight loss, I think it's important to address cravings, binge eating and emotional eating. These are common issues I see with my weight-loss clients, and it's important you educate yourself in what they mean.

A common question I get from clients is about cravings. Whether you're eating low-calorie or following another way of eating, feeling hungry all the time means something and it's important you listen to that. There are many reasons for cravings. The first one to consider is something I spoke about earlier—eating too few calories. When you eat below your body's RMR for a long period of time, resting metabolism can lower, leading to increased hunger over time. This is the most common reason I see for cravings among dieters.

Other reasons for cravings include skipping meals, being sleep deprived, enduring chronic stress, over-exercising, drinking too much caffeine and consuming too much added sugar. Not eating enough nonstarchy vegetables can also lead to cravings as the body becomes deficient in essential vitamins and minerals. Most individuals are not eating the daily recommended amounts of vegetables.

Additionally, having a weekly meal plan prepared in advance and sticking to a consistent routine of eating at regular intervals throughout the day can prevent cravings by keeping your blood sugar balanced. Another reason to prioritize meal planning!

As a note, breakfast is an important meal as it sets the stage for cravings later in the day. Eating a high-protein, high-vegetable breakfast is shown to reduce cravings and reduce daily calorie consumption.

BINGEING AND EMOTIONAL EATING

As I've worked with my weight-loss clients, my experience has been that many of them have created patterns around food and emotions leading to binge eating and emotional eating behaviors. When they feel anxious, depressed, stressed, lonely or bored, they often use food as a coping mechanism. They also eat food to avoid situations or people they don't want to deal with.

Using food to deal with these emotions is an unhealthy, deep-rooted behavior. These emotions should be addressed by a professional. I find emotional eaters who need to lose weight usually believe a new diet plan or way of eating will solve their bingeing and emotional eating problems; however, a new diet plan does not fix emotional eating. By the time my clients work with me, they're confused and frustrated that they wasted time and money doing things that didn't result in weight loss. This is because they were focusing on nutrition and exercise and not addressing the emotional and psychological behaviors driving them to overeat.

Getting the right help is not a sign of weakness—rather, it's an act of empowerment. Empower yourself to get the right nutrition knowledge as well as the right accountability, support and mindset coaching from an expert. You're worth it! Your health is too important to wait for the perfect time to start. There is never a perfect time to start. Taking imperfect action toward a goal is always better than doing nothing.

The low-calorie recipes in this book are a great tool to help you start your journey. My journey began with walking ten minutes a day, and it led me to losing 80 pounds (36 kg) and writing this cookbook. Imagine where you could be in a year if today you started making one recipe or adding one vegetable to your meal. This is your time, and the opportunities are endless!

HIGH-PROTEIN BREAKFASTS

Starting your day with a high-protein breakfast is shown to reduce cravings because it stabilizes blood sugar. Studies show those who start their day with a high-sugar breakfast eat more calories throughout the day than those who eat higher protein breakfasts. These breakfast recipes are high in protein, and they aren't your average boring diet foods. They're filled with flavor, packed with interesting textures and guaranteed to keep you fuller than traditional breakfast recipes. From pancakes to oats to eggs to smoothies, there's enough variety in this chapter to keep you excited about breakfast.

CALORIES:

211

Serves: 6

GREEK YOGURT WAFFLES

These Greek yogurt waffles, made with oat flour and eggs, are a low-calorie, protein-rich breakfast. They're easy to make, fluffy and delicious!

2 large eggs

⅔ cup (190 g) plain nonfat Greek yogurt

1¼ cups (300 ml) unsweetened almond milk, low-fat milk or milk of choice

1 tsp pure vanilla extract

2 cups (180 g) oat flour

1 tbsp (12 g) baking powder

¼ tsp salt

Avocado oil spray

In a blender, combine the eggs, yogurt, milk, vanilla, flour, baking powder and salt. Blend until the ingredients are smooth. Remove the blender's lid, scrape down the sides of the jar and blend again.

Heat a waffle iron to medium heat and spray it liberally with the avocado oil spray.

Pour ½ cup (120 ml) of the batter into the center of the waffle iron. Close the waffle iron and cook the waffle for 2 minutes on each side. Check the waffle after 4 minutes to see if it is done. Gently remove the waffle from the waffle iron and set it aside on a wire baking rack to cool.

Spray the waffle iron again with the avocado oil spray, then repeat the preceding steps until the remaining batter is gone.

Refrigerate the waffles for up to 7 days or store in the freezer for up to 60 days.

Serving Size: ⅙ **Calories:** 211 **Protein:** 11.9 grams **Carbohydrates:** 28.9 grams **Fiber:** 4.3 grams **Sugar:** 1.2 grams **Fat:** 5.1 grams **Sat. Fat:** 1 gram

CALORIES:

133

Serves: 9

SHEET PAN BANANA–CHOCOLATE CHIP PANCAKES

Pancakes baked on a sheet pan are the perfect portion-controlled way to start your day! Naturally sweetened with bananas and cinnamon and made flourless with whole-grain oats, these low-calorie pancakes are rich in fiber, high in protein and have a few chocolate chips sprinkled on top.

Avocado oil spray

2 large eggs

2 small bananas

1 cup (240 ml) unsweetened almond milk, low-fat milk or milk of choice

1 tsp pure vanilla extract

2 cups (160 g) rolled oats

1 tsp baking powder

2 tbsp (22 g) mini chocolate chips

Preheat the oven to 350°F (177°C). Spray a 9 x 13–inch (23 x 33–cm) sheet pan with the avocado oil spray.

In a blender or food processor, combine the eggs, bananas, milk and vanilla. Blend until the ingredients are smooth. Add the oats and baking powder. Blend again until the batter is smooth. Pour the batter onto the sheet pan and sprinkle the top with the chocolate chips.

Bake for 15 minutes, or until a toothpick inserted into the center comes out clean. Remove from the oven and let it cool in the sheet pan for 10 minutes. Slice into nine bars and serve.

Store the pancakes in the refrigerator for up to 5 days or in the freezer for up to 30 days.

Serving Size: ⅑ **Calories:** 133 **Protein:** 4.6 grams **Carbohydrates:** 22.3 grams **Fiber:** 3.2 grams **Sugar:** 4.4 grams **Fat:** 3.9 grams **Sat. Fat:** 1.3 grams

PB&J DONUTS

Yes, you can make low-calorie donuts! These protein-packed PB&J donuts are made flourless with whole-grain oats and minimal added sugar. Peanut butter and blueberries give them their delectable PB&J flavor. Treat yourself to this secretly healthy breakfast.

Avocado oil spray

1½ cups (120 g) rolled oats

⅓ cup (64 g) coconut sugar

2 tsp (8 g) baking powder

1 large egg

½ cup (120 ml) unsweetened almond milk, low-fat milk or milk of choice

3 tbsp (45 g) coconut oil, melted

1 tsp pure vanilla extract

¼ cup (45 g) creamy unsalted, sugar-free peanut butter

½ tsp salt

½ cup (50 g) frozen blueberries, thawed

Preheat the oven to 350°F (177°C). Spray a donut pan with the avocado oil spray.

In a blender or food processor, combine the oats, sugar and baking powder. Blend for about 2 minutes, until the oats are broken up into a flour mixture. Add the egg, milk, coconut oil, vanilla, peanut butter and salt. Blend again, until the ingredients are smooth. Spoon the batter into each donut cavity, filling it halfway. Sprinkle the blueberries on top of the batter, dividing them evenly among each cavity.

Spoon the remaining batter over the blueberries.

Bake the donuts for 15 minutes, until they have risen and set up. Remove the donuts from the oven and let them cool in the pan for 10 minutes before carefully removing and serving the donuts.

Store the donuts in the refrigerator for up to 5 days or in the freezer for up to 30 days.

Serving Size: ⅑ Calories: 176 Protein: 4.6 grams Carbohydrates: 20.1 grams Fiber: 2.3 grams Sugar: 6.5 grams Fat: 9.8 grams Sat. Fat: 5 grams

SIMPLE EGG WHITE OATMEAL

Oatmeal is naturally a low-calorie food. Adding egg whites to oatmeal is a simple solution to increase the protein, making this easy breakfast more filling and satisfying.

1 cup (240 ml) unsweetened almond milk, low-fat milk or milk of choice

½ cup (40 g) quick oats

½ tsp ground cinnamon

¼ tsp ground nutmeg

2 large egg whites or ¼ cup (60 ml) liquid egg whites

To make the oatmeal on the stove, combine the milk, oats, cinnamon and nutmeg in a small saucepan over medium heat. Stir the ingredients and cook until the liquid bubbles. Cook the oatmeal for 5 to 8 minutes, until the liquid is absorbed.

Remove the saucepan from the heat, pour the egg whites into the saucepan and stir continuously for 1 to 2 minutes, until the egg whites are cooked. Do not stop stirring the eggs; otherwise they will scramble.

Serve the oatmeal immediately with toppings of your choice.

To make the oatmeal in the microwave, combine the milk, oats, cinnamon and nutmeg in a microwave-safe bowl. Microwave the oatmeal on high for 1½ minutes, or until the liquid is absorbed. You may need to stir the oatmeal after it cooks to help the milk absorb. Add the egg whites to the bowl and stir the oatmeal for 1 to 2 minutes, until the eggs are cooked and combined.

Serve the oatmeal immediately with toppings of your choice.

Serving Size: 1 **Calories:** 250 **Protein:** 15.3 grams **Carbohydrates:** 31.3 grams **Fiber:** 6.8 grams **Sugar:** 1.2 grams **Fat:** 5.9 grams **Sat. Fat:** 0.6 gram

CHEESY BROCCOLI QUINOA EGG MUFFINS

These egg muffins are loaded with two secret high-protein ingredients—cottage cheese and quinoa, lighter ingredients that boost the nutrient content while giving the muffins the perfect cheesy flavor. Meal prep these delicious egg muffins once and enjoy them for breakfast all week long!

Avocado oil spray
2 cups (480 ml) water
1 cup (170 g) quinoa
6 large egg whites
3 large eggs
½ cup (115 g) nonfat cottage cheese
¼ cup (30 g) shredded low-moisture Cheddar cheese
½ tsp garlic powder
½ tsp black pepper
¼ tsp salt
1 cup (175 g) raw broccoli florets

Preheat the oven to 350°F (177°C). Liberally grease a muffin pan with the avocado oil spray.

Heat the water in a medium saucepan over high heat and bring it to a boil. Add the quinoa, stir it into the water and reduce the heat to low. Cover the quinoa and cook it for 10 minutes, or until the water is absorbed. Set the quinoa aside to cool completely.

In a large bowl, whisk together the egg whites, eggs, cottage cheese, Cheddar cheese, garlic powder, black pepper and salt. Add the broccoli florets and quinoa.

Fill each muffin cavity three-quarters full, distributing the mixture evenly among the cavities.

Bake the muffins for 22 to 25 minutes, until the eggs are fully cooked through.

Remove the muffins from the oven and let them cool in the pan for 5 minutes. Remove the muffins from the pan and serve.

Store the muffins in the refrigerator for up to 5 days.

Serving Size: ½ **Calories:** 101 **Protein:** 7.2 grams **Carbohydrates:** 12.8 grams **Fiber:** 1.9 grams **Sugar:** 0.7 gram **Fat:** 2.1 grams **Sat. Fat:** 0.5 gram

CALORIES:

345

BERRYLICIOUS CINNAMON CAULIFLOWER OATS

Start your day with an energizing bowl of cauliflower oatmeal naturally sweetened with berries and cinnamon! This waist-friendly breakfast is made lower in calories by adding cauliflower rice. An undetectable vegetable that adds fiber, cauliflower makes your oats thicker and more nutritious without adding more calories.

Serves: 1

½ cup (50 g) cauliflower rice (see notes)

½ cup (40 g) quick oats

3 tbsp (33 g) vanilla protein powder (see notes)

¼ cup (61 g) applesauce

1 cup (240 ml) unsweetened almond milk, low-fat milk or milk of choice

1 tsp ground cinnamon

½ cup (50 g) fresh mixed berries

In a small saucepan over medium heat, combine the cauliflower rice, oats, protein powder, applesauce, milk and cinnamon. Cook, stirring, for 3 to 4 minutes, until the mixture becomes thick and has the consistency of oatmeal.

Transfer the cauliflower oats to a serving bowl, stir in the berries and serve. This recipe can also be made as overnight oats and enjoyed cold or heated in a microwave for 1 to 2 minutes the next day.

NOTES

I recommend using frozen cauliflower rice. It has a milder taste than raw cauliflower rice. Thaw and strain the cauliflower rice before cooking.

Use a low-carb protein powder with no added sugar. My favorite brands are Garden of Life, Vega Clean and Orgain. The nutrition stats for this recipe are based on Garden of Life.

Serving Size: 1 **Calories:** 345 **Protein:** 23.9 grams **Carbohydrates:** 45.7 grams **Fiber:** 11.9 grams **Sugar:** 9.1 grams **Fat:** 7.5 grams **Sat. Fat:** 0.5 gram

CALORIES:

363

PISTACHIO-KALE POWER SMOOTHIE

This protein-packed smoothie is a light and filling breakfast balanced with pistachios, protein and kale. The pistachios add healthy fat to the smoothie to boost your fullness. They also add a hint of nutty flavor. Use this recipe to have breakfast ready in five minutes with minimal ingredients!

Serves: 1

1 small banana

1 cup (67 g) loosely packed kale

1 cup (240 ml) unsweetened almond milk, low-fat milk or milk of choice

2 tbsp (16 g) raw pistachios

½ cup (88 g) vanilla protein powder (see note)

½ cup (350 g) ice

In a blender, combine the banana, kale, milk, pistachios, protein powder and ice. Blend on high for 1 to 2 minutes until the ingredients are smooth and serve.

NOTE

Use a low-carb protein powder with no added sugar. My favorite brands are Garden of Life, Vega Clean and Orgain. The nutrition stats for this recipe are based on Garden of Life.

Serving Size: 1 **Calories:** 363 **Protein:** 28.9 grams **Carbohydrates:** 35.6 grams **Fiber:** 8 grams **Sugar:** 14.9 grams **Fat:** 14.4 grams **Sat. Fat:** 4.5 grams

CHOCOLATE AND PEANUT BUTTER MILKSHAKE

This five-ingredient milkshake is secretly good for you. Made with cottage cheese, peanut butter and whole-grain oats, these low-calorie ingredients give this smoothie its thick and creamy "milkshake" taste!

Serves: 2

1 cup (230 g) low-fat cottage cheese

2 tbsp (14 g) unsweetened cocoa powder

2 tbsp (22 g) creamy unsalted, sugar-free peanut butter or nut butter of choice

½ cup (40 g) rolled oats

½ cup (350 g) ice

Stevia, as needed

In a blender, combine the cottage cheese, cocoa powder, peanut butter, oats, ice and stevia. Blend on high for 1 to 2 minutes until the ingredients are smooth and serve.

Serving Size: ½ **Calories:** 269 **Protein:** 19.5 grams **Carbohydrates:** 29.6 grams **Fiber:** 5.5 grams **Sugar:** 4.5 grams **Fat:** 11.1 grams **Sat. Fat:** 2.4 grams

PUMPKIN-CINNAMON BREAKFAST MUFFINS

These healthy breakfast muffins are made lower in calories with one magical ingredient: pumpkin! They're lightly sweetened with cinnamon and coconut sugar and higher in protein than other muffins. They are a delicious, nutritionally balanced treat to start your day.

Serves: 8

Avocado oil spray (optional)

3 large eggs

⅓ cup (75 g) pumpkin puree

⅓ cup (64 g) coconut sugar

½ tsp pure vanilla extract

1 cup (80 g) rolled oats

1 cup (96 g) almond flour

1 tsp ground cinnamon

½ tsp baking powder

½ tsp baking soda

½ tsp salt

¼ cup (60 g) coconut oil, melted

Preheat the oven to 350°F (177°C). Prepare a muffin pan with muffin liners or spray the muffin cavities with the avocado oil spray.

In a medium bowl, combine the eggs, pumpkin puree, coconut sugar and vanilla. Whisk until the eggs are broken down and the mixture is smooth.

Fold in the oats, flour, cinnamon, baking powder, baking soda and salt. Then stir in the coconut oil.

Fill the muffin cavities with 2½ tablespoons (38 ml) of the batter, filling the cavities three-quarters full.

Bake the muffins for 25 minutes, or until a toothpick inserted into the center comes out clean.

Remove the muffins from the oven and let them cool in the muffin pan for 5 minutes. Transfer the muffins to a wire baking rack to cool completely.

Store in the refrigerator for up to 7 days or in the freezer for up to 60 days.

Serving Size: ⅛ **Calories:** 247 **Protein:** 7 grams **Carbohydrates:** 20.8 grams **Fiber:** 3.7 grams **Sugar:** 1 gram **Fat:** 5.1 grams **Sat. Fat:** 1 gram

KALE, SAUSAGE AND SWEET POTATO BREAKFAST HASH

Start your day with a simple breakfast like this hash. It's high in protein and balanced in healthy fat and carbs to keep you full all morning long—a great alternative to morning eggs!

Serves: 1

Olive oil spray

½ cup (63 g) diced sweet potato or yam

Salt, as needed

Black pepper, as needed

1 cup (67 g) coarsely chopped kale

1 link precooked nitrate- and sugar-free chicken sausage, diced

1 large egg

Spray a small skillet with the olive oil spray. Heat the skillet over medium heat. Add the sweet potato and sprinkle it with the salt and black pepper. Cover the skillet and cook the sweet potato for 8 minutes, until it is soft.

When the sweet potato is soft, add the kale to the skillet. Sauté the mixture for 3 to 4 minutes, until the kale is wilted, then stir in the chicken sausage.

Make a well in the center of the skillet. Crack the egg into the well. Cover the skillet and cook the hash for 3 minutes, until the egg is set.

Remove the hash from the skillet and serve immediately.

Serving Size: 1 **Calories:** 304 **Protein:** 19.6 grams **Carbohydrates:** 30.3 grams **Fiber:** 5.9 grams **Sugar:** 18.4 grams **Fat:** 12.2 grams **Sat. Fat:** 2.7 grams

CALORIES:

143

SPINACH-MUSHROOM QUICHE WITH POTATO CRUST

This easy quiche recipe replaces flour with sweet potatoes for a lighter crust. Sweet potatoes are naturally low in calories and high in vitamins and minerals. They make the perfect crust to hold the yummy spinach-mushroom filling. This quiche is a healthier breakfast recipe to serve for a light brunch.

Serves: 6

Avocado oil spray

2 cups (300 g) 1-inch (2.5-cm)-thick slices peeled Japanese sweet potatoes

Salt, as needed

Black pepper, as needed

¼ cup (38 g) diced white onion

2 cups (60 g) fresh baby spinach

8 large eggs

¼ cup (60 ml) unsweetened almond milk, low-fat milk or milk of choice

½ tsp garlic powder

⅓ cup (25 g) thinly sliced white button mushrooms

Preheat the oven to 425°F (218°C). Spray a 9½-inch (24-cm) pie dish with the avocado oil spray. Place the sweet potatoes in the pie dish, arranging them in an even layer on the bottom and around the sides. (They can overlap a bit and can have spaces between them as the egg mixture will hold everything together after it bakes.)

Spray the sweet potato crust with avocado oil spray and sprinkle it with the salt and black pepper. Bake the crust for 20 minutes, until the sweet potatoes are soft.

While the crust bakes, spray a large skillet with avocado oil spray, then add the onion and spinach and bring the heat to medium. Cook the mixture for 2 to 3 minutes, until the onion is translucent and the spinach is wilted. Turn off the heat and set the skillet aside.

Remove the sweet potatoes from the oven and reduce the heat to 400°F (204°C).

In a large bowl, whisk together the eggs, milk, garlic powder, salt and black pepper until the ingredients are smooth. Add the onion and spinach to the mixture, then pour it over the sweet potato crust. Arrange the mushrooms on top of the filling.

Bake the quiche for 25 minutes, until the center is set. Remove it from the oven and let it cool for 5 minutes, then slice it into six portions.

Serving Size: ⅙ **Calories:** 143 **Protein:** 9.7 grams **Carbohydrates:** 10.9 grams **Fiber:** 1.8 grams **Sugar:** 2.4 grams **Fat:** 6.5 grams **Sat. Fat:** 2.1 grams

CALORIES:

136

CHEESY TEX-MEX CAULIFLOWER CASSEROLE

This nourishing egg casserole is packed with cauliflower rice, salsa and Tex-Mex flavors! Cauliflower rice is the perfect accompaniment for eggs. It is naturally low in calories, filling, has a mild taste and boosts the nutrient content. And it makes for a Mexican-style breakfast casserole that tastes so good you won't believe it's low-calorie.

Serves: 6

Avocado oil spray
6 large eggs
10 large egg whites
½ cup (130 g) salsa
½ tsp chili powder
½ tsp garlic powder
¼ tsp ground cumin
Salt, as needed
Black pepper, as needed
2 cups (200 g) cauliflower rice
1 small jalapeño, thinly sliced
¼ cup (30 g) shredded low-moisture Cheddar cheese

Preheat the oven to 400°F (204°C). Spray an 8½ x 5½–inch (21 x 14–cm) baking dish with the avocado oil spray.

In a large bowl, whisk together the eggs, egg whites, salsa, chili powder, garlic powder, cumin, salt and black pepper. Stir in the cauliflower rice and pour the mixture into the prepared baking dish.

Place the jalapeño slices on top and sprinkle the casserole with the Cheddar cheese.

Bake the casserole for 40 to 45 minutes, until the top is golden brown and the center is fully set. Check halfway through the cooking to ensure the top is not burning—if the top is browning too quickly, cover it with foil and continue baking.

Remove the casserole from the oven and let cool for 10 minutes in the baking dish. Slice it into six large pieces and serve.

Store leftovers in the refrigerator for up to 5 days.

NOTE
Use frozen cauliflower rice. Thaw and strain before adding to the recipe.

Serving Size: ⅙ Calories: 136 Protein: 14.9 grams Carbohydrates: 4.2 grams Fiber: 0.8 gram Sugar: 2 grams Fat: 6.6 grams Sat. Fat: 2.6 grams

FLOURLESS COCOA PROTEIN PANCAKES

These chocolate pancakes are higher in protein thanks to cottage cheese and egg whites. They're made with whole-grain oats, making them more filling than traditional flour-based pancakes. You can't go wrong starting your day with this fluffy, low-calorie stack!

Serves: 14

Avocado oil spray, optional

2 cups (160 g) rolled oats

12 large egg whites (see notes)

¼ cup (28 g) unsweetened cocoa powder

16 oz (450 g) low-fat cottage cheese

2 tsp (6 g) ground cinnamon

½ tsp baking powder

Preheat a large nonstick skillet over medium-low heat. (If your skillet requires greasing, spray it with avocado oil spray.)

In a blender or food processor, combine the oats, egg whites, cocoa powder, cottage cheese, cinnamon and baking powder. Blend until the ingredients are smooth, then ladle ¼ cup (60 ml) of the batter into the skillet to form one pancake. Repeat this process until the bottom of the skillet is full. Cook the pancakes for 3 to 4 minutes, until the tops are bubbly, then flip them and cook them for 3 to 4 minutes. Transfer the pancakes to a wire baking rack to cool as you cook the remaining batter.

Serve the pancakes immediately or store them in the refrigerator for up to 10 days or in the freezer for up to 60 days.

NOTES

You may substitute six whole eggs for the egg whites. Note that this substitution will significantly increase the calories.

These pancakes are unsweetened and are best served with a touch of real maple syrup and fruit.

Serving Size: ¹⁄₁₄ **Calories:** 90 **Protein:** 8.4 grams **Carbohydrates:** 12.7 grams **Fiber:** 2.2 grams **Sugar:** 0.9 gram **Fat:** 1.4 grams **Sat. Fat:** 0.3 gram

CALORIES:

190

TWO-MINUTE ENGLISH MUFFIN

This two-minute English muffin is made easily in a microwave. Pumpkin replaces the oil, making this muffin a healthier, low-calorie alternative to flour-based English muffins. It also has no added sugar, which is commonly found in store-bought breads. This English muffin is great for making egg sandwiches or enjoying with fresh jam on top.

Serves: 1

2 tbsp (28 g) pumpkin puree

2 tbsp (30 ml) unsweetened almond milk, low-fat milk or milk of choice, plus more as needed

⅓ cup (27 g) rolled oats

1 tbsp (10 g) chia seeds

½ tsp baking powder

¼ tsp salt

Avocado oil spray

In a small bowl, stir together the pumpkin puree and milk. Set the bowl aside.

In a blender, combine the oats, chia seeds, baking powder and salt. Blend for 1 minute, or until the oat mixture forms a flour. Add the flour mixture to the pumpkin mixture and stir. If the ingredients are too dry, add ½ teaspoon of milk at a time until it is no longer dry. The mixture should be spongy and sticky.

Spray a cereal bowl with the avocado oil spray. Add the muffin mixture and flatten it with a spatula. Microwave the muffin mixture for 2 minutes, or until the muffin has risen. Remove the muffin from the microwave and let it cool in the bowl for 5 minutes. Gently remove it from the bowl with a spatula. Transfer the muffin to a cutting board and let it stand for 5 minutes (or until it is completely cool) before slicing it in half.

Toast the English muffin in a toaster or under a broiler, spread your favorite topping on top of the muffin and serve.

NOTE

Alternatively, you can bake the muffin. Use an oven-safe bowl and bake the muffin in a preheated 350°F (177°C) oven for 12 to 15 minutes.

Serving Size: 1 **Calories:** 190 **Protein:** 6.6 grams **Carbohydrates:** 30 grams **Fiber:** 8.2 grams **Sugar:** 1 gram **Fat:** 6.2 grams **Sat. Fat:** 0.3 gram

LIGHT SOUPS, SALADS AND LUNCHES

The recipes in this chapter are easy to make for meal prep or low-calorie lunches. They're made with healthier, more nutritious ingredients that fill you up and satisfy you while keeping the calories low.

Many of these are classic recipes that have been lightened up. They include the right amount of protein and vegetables to keep your blood sugar stable and keep cravings away, yet they're just as delicious as the real deal. Enjoy!

MOROCCAN SPICED TUNA SALAD

This Moroccan spiced tuna salad is made with fresh ingredients and bursting with flavor. It's higher in protein and lower in calories compared to mayo-based tuna salads because it replaces mayo with Greek yogurt. It's an easy, ten-minute lunch that requires minimal effort!

Serves: 2

½ cup (143 g) plain nonfat Greek yogurt

1 tbsp (15 g) tahini

1 tbsp (16 g) Dijon mustard

½ tsp ground cumin

½ tsp ground cinnamon

½ tsp ground turmeric

½ tsp black pepper

10 oz (280 g) canned tuna in water, drained

¼ cup (30 g) low-sugar dried cranberries

1 large head butter or iceberg lettuce or greens of choice

1 green onion, diced

In a large bowl, combine the yogurt, tahini, mustard, cumin, cinnamon, turmeric and black pepper. Mix until the dressing is smooth. Fold in the tuna and dried cranberries.

Serve the tuna salad in lettuce leaves as wraps or over greens as a salad with the green onion sprinkled on top of the tuna.

Serving Size: ½ **Calories:** 346 **Protein:** 43.3 grams **Carbohydrates:** 18.3 grams **Fiber:** 2.6 grams **Sugar:** 12.8 grams **Fat:** 10.5 grams **Sat. Fat:** 1.6 grams

CALORIES:

172

EVERYTHING BUT THE BAGEL CHICKEN SALAD

This delicious mayo-free chicken salad is made with Greek yogurt in place of mayo. Chopped veggies and everything bagel seasoning adds texture and flavor without the calories, yielding a healthier chicken salad with tons of flavor that's perfect for an easy lunch to take with you or to enjoy for a quick lunch at home.

Serves: 3

3 (15-oz [420-g]) cans chicken in water, drained

½ cup (143 g) plain nonfat Greek yogurt

1 tbsp (15 ml) fresh lemon juice

½ cup (50 g) diced celery

½ cup (25 g) shredded carrots

1 tbsp (10 g) everything bagel seasoning

½ tsp black pepper

6 leaves red cabbage

In a large bowl, combine the chicken, yogurt, lemon juice, celery, carrots, everything bagel seasoning and black pepper. Stir to combine. Serve the chicken salad in cabbage leaf "cups."

Serving Size: ⅓ **Calories:** 172 **Protein:** 18.2 grams **Carbohydrates:** 17.8 grams **Fiber:** 4.8 grams **Sugar:** 10 grams **Fat:** 1.7 grams **Sat. Fat:** 0 grams

OPEN-FACED TUNA MELT

This healthier tuna melt uses Greek yogurt and mustard in place of mayo to make the dish higher in protein and lower in fat. It cooks in ten minutes and tastes like the real thing.

2 slices organic whole-grain bread

Avocado oil spray

15 oz (420 g) canned tuna in water, drained

⅓ cup (95 g) plain nonfat Greek yogurt

1 tbsp (16 g) yellow mustard

1 tsp apple cider vinegar

½ tsp garlic powder

¼ cup (25 g) diced celery

2 tsp (1 g) minced fresh dill

¼ cup (30 g) shredded low-moisture Cheddar cheese

Preheat the oven broiler to high. Line a small baking sheet with parchment paper. Place the bread on the baking sheet. Spray the top of the bread slices with the avocado oil spray. Broil the bread for 3 to 4 minutes, until it is brown and crispy.

Remove the baking sheet from the oven and set it aside. Reduce the broiler to low.

In a medium bowl, mix together the tuna, yogurt, mustard, vinegar, garlic powder and celery.

Spoon half of the tuna salad mixture on each slice of bread. Sprinkle the dill over the tuna mixture, followed by the Cheddar cheese.

Broil the open-faced sandwiches for 2 minutes to melt the cheese. Remove the tuna melts from the oven and serve them immediately.

Serving Size: ½ **Calories:** 228 **Protein:** 21.7 grams **Carbohydrates:** 25.6 grams **Fiber:** 5.6 grams **Sugar:** 6.6 grams **Fat:** 4.9 grams **Sat. Fat:** 1.3 grams

BUFFALO-PARMESAN CHICKEN NUGGETS

Never miss breaded chicken again! These chicken nuggets have a crispy oat-Parmesan crust and a kick of heat. This is a better-for-you breaded chicken recipe that's made with fewer calories, boasts nutritious ingredients and is kid-approved. Serve these nuggets for lunch with your favorite veggie as a side or as a healthy appetizer.

Serves: 4

1 cup (80 g) rolled oats

1½ tbsp (23 ml) extra-virgin olive oil

2 tbsp (30 ml) hot sauce, plus more as needed

¼ cup (45 g) grated Parmesan cheese

½ tsp garlic powder

½ tsp paprika

¼ tsp cayenne pepper

⅛ tsp black pepper

1 lb (450 g) boneless, skinless chicken breasts, cut into 1-inch (2.5-cm) pieces

Avocado oil spray

Preheat the oven to 425°F (218°C). Line a 15¼ x 10¼-inch (38 x 26-cm) baking sheet with parchment paper.

Pulse the oats in a blender until they have a breadcrumb consistency.

In a small bowl, mix together the oil and hot sauce. In a medium bowl, mix together the oats, Parmesan cheese, garlic powder, paprika, cayenne pepper and black pepper.

Dip a piece of the chicken into the olive oil–hot sauce mixture then immediately into the oat-Parmesan mixture, coating it generously. Place the piece of chicken on the prepared baking sheet. Repeat this process for the remaining chicken pieces.

Lightly spray the chicken nuggets with the avocado oil spray. Bake the chicken for 8 minutes.

Flip the chicken nuggets and bake them for 5 more minutes, or until they are crispy and brown.

Serve the chicken nuggets immediately with additional hot sauce and veggies.

Serving Size: ¼ **Calories:** 340 **Protein:** 40.2 grams **Carbohydrates:** 17.2 grams **Fiber:** 2.7 grams **Sugar:** 0.1 gram **Fat:** 12.1 grams **Sat. Fat:** 3 grams

238

Serves: 4

SPICY CHIPOTLE-LIME SALMON

This easy baked salmon is drenched in a homemade chipotle sauce that's low-calorie and bursting with garlic and lime flavors, an easy way to guarantee your salmon is delicious every time. Serve this dish with your favorite veggies and rice for a deliciously light meal.

Avocado oil spray

1½-lb (675-g) wild-caught salmon fillet

1 tbsp (15 ml) olive oil

¼ cup (60 ml) fresh lime juice

1 chipotle chili in adobo sauce

1 tbsp (15 ml) adobo sauce

¼ cup (8 g) fresh cilantro leaves

2 tsp (6 g) minced garlic

½ tsp ground cumin

1 small lime, thinly sliced, plus more as needed

1 jalapeño, sliced

Preheat the oven to 375°F (191°C). Line a 15¼ x 10¼-inch (38 x 26-cm) baking sheet with foil. Spray the foil with the avocado oil spray.

Place the salmon on the foil and pat it dry with a paper towel. Set the salmon aside.

In a blender, combine the oil, lime juice, chipotle chili, adobo sauce, cilantro, garlic and cumin. Blend for 1 to 2 minutes, until the ingredients are smooth.

Spoon the sauce evenly over the salmon and top it with the lime slices. Cover the salmon with another piece of foil. Pinch the edges of the foil together to form a sealed packet, leaving room for the salmon to steam in the packet.

Bake the salmon for 20 minutes. Check the salmon; it should be almost completely cooked through at the thickest part. Cooking times will vary depending on the thickness of the salmon. Do not let the salmon cook too long, as it can progress to overcooked very quickly.

Remove the salmon from the oven and open the foil so the fish is uncovered. Increase the oven's temperature to a high broil. Broil the salmon for 2 minutes to crisp the top.

Remove the salmon from the oven and serve it warm with sliced limes as needed and the jalapeño.

Serving Size: ¼ **Calories:** 238 **Protein:** 29 grams **Carbohydrates:** 2.3 grams **Fiber:** 0.1 gram **Sugar:** 0.2 gram **Fat:** 12 grams **Sat. Fat:** 1.8 grams

66 THE LOW-CALORIE **COOKBOOK**

GREEK CHICKEN BURGERS WITH TZATZIKI

These baked Greek chicken burgers are a fusion of classic Mediterranean flavors. Lighter and healthier than a traditional burger and served bunless with a homemade Greek yogurt tzatziki sauce, these burgers are a simple meal you can make in less than thirty minutes.

Serves: 4

GREEK YOGURT TZATZIKI

1 cup (285 g) plain nonfat Greek yogurt

½ cup (75 g) finely chopped cucumber

2 tbsp (30 ml) lemon juice

1 tsp minced fresh dill

½ tsp (5 g) minced garlic

BURGERS

1 lb (450 g) ground chicken

1 tbsp (15 ml) extra-virgin olive oil

⅓ cup (50 g) diced red onion

½ cup (112 g) thawed frozen spinach

¼ cup (80 g) diced roasted red bell peppers

¼ cup (38 g) crumbled feta cheese

1 tsp minced garlic

1 tsp dried oregano

Salt, as needed

Black pepper, as needed

Vegetables or lettuce wraps, for serving

To make the Greek yogurt tzatziki, mix together the yogurt, cucumber, lemon juice, dill and garlic in a medium bowl. Place the tzatziki in the refrigerator to chill while you prepare the burgers.

To make the burgers, preheat the oven to 350°F (177°C). Line a medium baking sheet with parchment paper.

In a large bowl, combine the chicken, oil, onion, spinach, red bell peppers, feta cheese, garlic, oregano, salt and black pepper. Use your hands to mix the ingredients together thoroughly. Divide the meat into four equal portions. Shape each portion into a burger and place it on the prepared baking sheet.

Bake the burgers for 25 minutes. Increase the oven's temperature to a high broil. Broil for 5 minutes to make the burgers crispy.

Remove the burgers from the oven and serve them with vegetables or in lettuce wraps with the tzatziki sauce on top.

Serving Size: ¼ **Calories:** 294 **Protein:** 31.3 grams **Carbohydrates:** 7.7 grams **Fiber:** 1.4 grams **Sugar:** 4 grams **Fat:** 16.1 grams **Sat. Fat:** 4.8 grams

SRIRACHA SHRIMP CAESAR SALAD

A Caesar salad can be made lighter with a few simple swaps! This recipe uses Greek yogurt and Parmesan to create an amazing, light dressing in just five minutes. The Caesar dressing tops juicy, baked shrimp drizzled in Sriracha and garlic over a bed of greens. This is a simple salad that's high in protein and has many flavors with fewer calories!

Serves: 3

CAESAR DRESSING

½ cup (143 g) plain nonfat Greek yogurt

¼ cup (45 g) grated Parmesan cheese

1 tbsp (15 ml) extra-virgin olive oil

2 tbsp (30 ml) fresh lemon juice

2 tbsp (30 ml) water

1 tsp Dijon mustard

2 anchovies in water, drained

SALAD

1 lb (450 g) shrimp, tails removed and deveined

2 tbsp (18 g) minced garlic

2 tbsp (30 ml) Sriracha sauce

4½ cups (135 g) mixed greens

1 cup (150 g) grape tomatoes, halved

To make the Caesar dressing, combine the yogurt, Parmesan cheese, oil, lemon juice, water, mustard and anchovies in a high-speed blender. Blend until the ingredients are homogenous. Place the dressing in the refrigerator to chill.

To make the salad, preheat the oven to 350°F (177°C). Line a medium baking sheet with parchment paper.

In a large bowl, combine the shrimp, garlic and Sriracha. Transfer the shrimp to the prepared baking sheet, spreading them out evenly. Drizzle the remaining garlic and Sriracha in the bowl over the shrimp.

Bake the shrimp for 10 minutes, until they are opaque.

Serve the shrimp over the mixed greens with the grape tomatoes and Caesar dressing.

If you are meal prepping this recipe, keep the dressing and shrimp separate until you are ready to eat.

Serving Size: ⅓ **Calories:** 280 **Protein:** 40.5 grams **Carbohydrates:** 12 grams **Fiber:** 1.5 grams **Sugar:** 5.8 grams **Fat:** 8.1 grams **Sat. Fat:** 1.9 grams

CALORIES:

470

MEDITERRANEAN KALE SALMON SALAD

This Mediterranean kale salmon salad is packed with protein, healthy fat, veggies and a delicious, lightened-up red wine vinaigrette—a healthy balance of nutrients to keep you full and satisfied. This tasty salad is great for a quick lunch or dinner!

Serves: 2

SALAD

2 (4-oz [112-g]) salmon fillets

Salt, as needed

Black pepper, as needed

6 cups (402 g) finely chopped kale

1 cup (150 g) diced cucumber

⅓ cup (50 g) diced red onion

⅓ cup (18 g) oil-packed sun-dried tomatoes, drained and diced

½ cup (56 g) pepperoncini, diced

¼ cup (38 g) crumbled feta cheese

⅓ cup (20 g) finely chopped fresh parsley

DRESSING

2 tbsp (30 ml) red wine vinegar

2 tbsp (30 ml) extra-virgin olive oil

1 tsp fresh lemon juice

1 tsp dried oregano

1 tsp dried parsley

½ tsp black pepper

To make the salad, preheat the oven to 350°F (177°C). Line a small baking sheet with parchment paper.

Place the salmon fillets skin-side down on the prepared baking sheet. Sprinkle the salt and black pepper over the salmon. Bake the salmon for 25 to 30 minutes, until the fish flakes easily with a fork.

While the salmon bakes, make the dressing. In a small bowl, whisk together the vinegar, oil, lemon juice, oregano, parsley and black pepper.

To assemble the salad, place the kale in a large bowl and drizzle the dressing over the kale. Massage the kale with your hands to distribute the dressing. Add the cucumber, onion, tomatoes, pepperoncini, feta cheese and parsley. Divide the salad between two bowls.

Remove the salmon from the oven and shred it with a fork, discarding the skin. Place the shredded salmon on top of the salad and serve. If you are meal prepping this recipe, store the salmon separate from the salad and dressing.

Serving Size: ½ **Calories:** 470 **Protein:** 37.1 grams **Carbohydrates:** 36.2 grams **Fiber:** 8.1 grams **Sugar:** 8.4 grams **Fat:** 21.1 grams **Sat. Fat:** 5.7 grams

BUFFALO CHICKEN TACO SALAD WITH AVOCADO DRESSING

This juicy and flavorful buffalo chicken taco salad is baked in a low-calorie marinade made from hot sauce and spices. You'll love this hearty and healthy salad, served over greens with a sprinkle of blue cheese, pico de gallo and a light avocado dressing.

Serves: 3

SALAD

3 (4-oz [112-g]) boneless, skinless chicken breasts

¼ cup (60 ml) hot sauce

1 tbsp (15 ml) fresh lime juice

1 tbsp (15 ml) honey

1 tsp garlic powder

1 tsp chili powder

½ tsp ground cumin

½ tsp paprika

½ tsp onion powder

6 cups (450 g) coarsely chopped romaine lettuce

¼ cup (38 g) crumbled blue cheese

¾ cup (185 g) pico de gallo

DRESSING

1 small avocado, peeled and pitted

½ cup (120 ml) water, plus more if needed

¼ cup (60 ml) fresh lime juice

¼ tsp ground cumin

½ tsp salt

To make the salad, place the chicken in a medium baking dish. Set the baking dish aside.

In a small bowl, combine the hot sauce, lime juice, honey, garlic powder, chili powder, cumin, paprika and onion powder. Pour three-quarters of the marinade over the chicken. Marinate the chicken for 2 hours, or overnight, in the refrigerator.

Preheat the oven to 375°F (191°C). Bake the chicken for 30 minutes, until its internal temperature reaches 165°F (74°C). Increase the oven's temperature to a high broil and broil the chicken for 5 minutes to make the chicken crispy. Remove the chicken from the oven, brush the remaining marinade over the chicken and set the chicken aside for 10 minutes.

To make the dressing, combine the avocado, water, lime juice, cumin and salt in a blender. Blend until the ingredients are smooth. If desired, add more water to the dressing to thin it out. Set the dressing aside.

To assemble the salads, place the lettuce in bowls and add the blue cheese and pico de gallo. Slice the chicken and top the salad with it. Drizzle the salads with the dressing and serve. If you are meal prepping this recipe, store the chicken separately from the salad and dressing.

Serving Size: ⅓ **Calories:** 368 **Protein:** 39.7 grams **Carbohydrates:** 21.6 grams **Fiber:** 7 grams **Sugar:** 11.3 grams **Fat:** 14.6 grams **Sat. Fat:** 4.2 grams

THAI TURKEY BURRITO BOWLS WITH QUINOA

These burrito bowls are made with Thai-spiced ground turkey, an array of cooked vegetables, greens and quinoa. The ingredients are lighter compared to takeout, as this dish uses less oil and more vegetables. These bowls are a low-calorie meal with interesting and delicious flavors.

2 cups (480 ml) water

1 cup (170 g) uncooked quinoa

2 tbsp (30 ml) olive oil

1 medium green bell pepper, thinly sliced

1 medium yellow bell pepper, thinly sliced

1 medium red bell pepper, thinly sliced

Salt, as needed

1½ cups (225 g) thinly sliced zucchini

1 lb (450 g) 93% lean ground turkey

1 tsp paprika

½ tsp ground turmeric

½ tsp ground coriander

½ tsp ground cumin

½ tsp mustard powder

¼ tsp ground ginger

Black pepper, as needed

⅔ cup (173 g) red salsa

8 cups (240 g) mixed greens, coarsely chopped

Diced jalapeños, as needed (optional)

Diced avocado, as needed (optional)

Coarsely chopped fresh cilantro, as needed (optional)

Heat the water in a medium saucepan over high heat and bring it to a boil. Add the quinoa, stir it into the water and reduce the heat to low. Cover the quinoa and cook it for 10 minutes, or until the water is absorbed. Set the quinoa aside to cool completely.

In a large skillet over medium heat, combine the oil, green bell pepper, yellow bell pepper and red bell pepper. Sprinkle the bell peppers with salt and cook them for 6 minutes. Add the zucchini, toss to combine it with the bell peppers and cook the mixture for 5 to 7 minutes, until the zucchini is soft. Remove the vegetables from the skillet and set them aside.

Add the turkey to the skillet and season it with the paprika, turmeric, coriander, cumin, mustard powder, ginger, salt and black pepper. Cook the turkey for 5 to 8 minutes, using a spatula to break up the meat as it browns.

Once the meat is cooked, stir in the salsa and assemble the burrito bowls by layering the mixed greens with the quinoa, cooked vegetables, turkey, jalapeños (if using), avocado (if using) and cilantro (if using).

Serving Size: ¼ **Calories:** 463 **Protein:** 31.3 grams **Carbohydrates:** 45.7 grams **Fiber:** 7.8 grams **Sugar:** 10.4 grams **Fat:** 18.5 grams **Sat. Fat:** 3.4 grams

CALORIES:

173

Serves: 5

HUMMUS TUNA CAKES

These hummus tuna cakes are so tasty, you won't believe they're low-calorie! Tuna is a naturally low-calorie, high-protein food. This recipe adds hummus and spices to boost the flavor of otherwise boring tuna. These cakes are a simple throw-together meal that's unbelievably delicious.

2 (8-oz [224-g]) cans tuna in water, drained

¼ cup (60 g) hummus

2 tbsp (32 g) Dijon mustard, plus more as needed

½ tsp garlic powder

½ tsp dried parsley

½ cup (40 g) rolled oats

1 tbsp (15 ml) extra-virgin olive oil

In a medium bowl, combine the tuna, hummus, mustard, garlic powder and parsley. Set the tuna mixture aside.

Place the oats in a blender. Blend for 1 to 2 minutes, until the oats form a flour. Add the oat flour to the tuna mixture and stir to combine.

Add the oil to a large skillet over medium heat. Scoop out ¼ cup (60 g) of the tuna mixture and place it in the skillet. Press the tuna down with a spatula and then pat any remnants that are loose back into the tuna cake. It will easily stick together. Repeat this process until you have 5 tuna patties.

Cook the tuna cakes for 5 minutes, then flip them and cook them for 5 more minutes, until they are crispy on both sides. You will know they are ready to flip when you see the bottom form a crust.

Remove the tuna cakes from the skillet and serve them immediately with your favorite vegetables and additional Dijon mustard for dipping. Alternatively, store them in the refrigerator for up to 7 days.

Serving Size: ⅕ **Calories:** 173 **Protein:** 24.1 grams **Carbohydrates:** 8.8 grams **Fiber:** 1.4 grams **Sugar:** 0 grams **Fat:** 4.2 grams **Sat. Fat:** 0.1 gram

CALORIES:

486

Serves: 4

HEALTHY CHICKEN PAD THAI

High in protein and fiber but low in calories, this healthy spin on chicken pad Thai is better for you than takeout. It combines spiralized sweet potato and an array of vegetables with a creamy lime–peanut butter sauce. You'll love this for an easy and filling meal!

SAUCE

½ cup (88 g) creamy unsalted, sugar-free peanut, sunflower, almond or cashew butter

½ cup (120 ml) water

1 tbsp (15 ml) honey

1 tbsp (15 ml) fresh lime juice

1 tbsp (15 ml) rice wine vinegar

2 tbsp (30 ml) coconut aminos or soy sauce

1 tsp garlic powder

1 tsp ground ginger

CHICKEN PAD THAI

1 lb (450 g) chicken breast tenders

1 tbsp (15 ml) extra-virgin olive oil

2 large egg whites

1 cup (175 g) diced red bell pepper

2 cups (100 g) julienned carrots

1 cup (100 g) coarsely chopped red cabbage

2 cups (300 g) spiralized sweet potato

2 tbsp (18 g) coarsely chopped raw cashews

¼ cup (8 g) coarsely chopped fresh cilantro

¼ cup (8 g) finely chopped green onions

To make the sauce, mix together the peanut butter, water, honey, lime juice, vinegar, coconut aminos, garlic powder and ginger in a medium bowl.

To make the pad Thai, add half of the sauce to a large skillet over medium heat. Add the chicken breast tenders. Cook the chicken breast tenders for 5 minutes, until their internal temperature reaches 165°F (74°C), then transfer them and the sauce to a plate and set the plate aside.

Add the oil and egg whites to the skillet. Cook the egg whites for 2 to 3 minutes, until they are scrambled, and transfer them to a separate plate and set the plate aside. Add the bell pepper, carrots, cabbage and sweet potato to the skillet. Cook the vegetables for 5 minutes, then add the chicken, remaining sauce and egg whites to the skillet. Toss to combine and cook the pad Thai for 5 minutes, or until the vegetables are al dente.

Serve the pad Thai with the cashews, cilantro, green onions and remaining sauce.

Store in the refrigerator for up to 5 days.

Serving Size: ¼ **Calories:** 486 **Protein:** 39.4 grams **Carbohydrates:** 37.1 grams **Fiber:** 7.1 grams **Sugar:** 16.2 grams **Fat:** 22.3 grams **Sat. Fat:** 4.2 grams

CALORIES:

269

Serves: 4

STUFFED PEPPER SOUP WITH CAULIFLOWER RICE

This healthy soup is filled with so much flavor and takes fewer than twenty minutes to make. An Italian-inspired soup that uses lean ingredients—ground turkey, peppers, onion, tomato sauce and cauliflower rice—this dish is a low-calorie, veggie-rich and protein-packed meal that's nourishing and family-approved!

2 tbsp (30 ml) extra-virgin olive oil

½ cup (75 g) diced white onion

¼ cup (36 g) minced garlic

1 lb (450 g) 99% lean ground turkey or chicken

1 cup (175 g) diced red bell pepper

1 cup (175 g) diced yellow bell pepper

1 cup (175 g) diced orange bell pepper

1 tbsp (3 g) Italian seasoning

1 tsp paprika

½ tsp chili powder

¼ tsp cayenne pepper

½ tsp salt

½ tsp black pepper

2 cups (480 ml) low-sodium chicken broth

15 oz (443 ml) canned tomato sauce

3 cups (300 g) cauliflower rice (see note)

Coarsely chopped fresh parsley, as needed (optional)

In a large pot over medium heat, combine the oil, onion and garlic. Sauté the onion and garlic for 5 minutes.

Add the turkey, red bell pepper, yellow bell pepper, orange bell pepper, Italian seasoning, paprika, chili powder, cayenne pepper, salt and black pepper. Use a spoon to break up the meat. Cook the mixture for 5 to 7 minutes, until the turkey has browned, then add the broth and tomato sauce. Bring the soup to a boil then immediately reduce the heat to low and simmer the soup. Add the cauliflower rice, stir, cover the pot and cook the soup for 15 minutes, until the cauliflower is tender.

Serve the soup immediately garnished with the parsley (if using).

Keep the soup in the refrigerator for up to 7 days or in the freezer for up to 60 days.

NOTE

I recommend using frozen cauliflower rice that is thawed and drained for this recipe.

Serving Size: ¼ **Calories:** 269 **Protein:** 30.5 grams **Carbohydrates:** 20 grams **Fiber:** 4.6 grams **Sugar:** 10 grams **Fat:** 8.9 grams **Sat. Fat:** 1.6 grams

CALORIES:

224

Serves: 6

CHEESEBURGER SOUP

This cheeseburger soup is a healthy spin on fast food, a rich bowl of comfort made with potatoes instead of the bun. Cauliflower is the secret ingredient that makes this soup thick and luxurious while keeping it lower in calories.

4 cups (428 g) coarsely chopped cauliflower

1 cup (240 ml) water

1 cup (240 ml) unsweetened almond milk, low-fat milk or milk of choice

1 tbsp (15 ml) extra-virgin olive oil

1 cup (100 g) diced celery

1 cup (150 g) thinly sliced carrots

½ cup (75 g) diced white onion

1 lb (450 g) 99% lean ground turkey or ground beef

2 cups (450 g) peeled and diced russet potatoes

1 tsp dried parsley

1 tsp dried basil

½ tsp salt

½ tsp black pepper

3 cups (720 ml) low-sodium chicken broth

2 tbsp (32 g) spicy mustard

1 tbsp (17 g) no-sugar-added ketchup

½ cup (60 g) shredded low-moisture Cheddar cheese

2 tbsp (4 g) finely chopped green onions

In a large pot over high heat, combine the cauliflower and water. Bring the water to a boil. Boil the cauliflower for 5 minutes, or until it is soft. Drain the cauliflower, then transfer it to a blender. Add the milk. Blend until the cauliflower is smooth.

Set the pot over medium heat. Add the oil, celery, carrots and white onion to the pot. Sauté the vegetables for 5 to 7 minutes, until they are soft. Add the turkey and cook for 5 minutes, breaking up the turkey with a spatula as it cooks.

When the turkey has browned, add the potatoes, parsley, basil, salt, black pepper and broth. Bring the mixture to a boil and cook for 5 minutes. Cover the pot and reduce the heat to a simmer. Cook the mixture for 20 minutes, until the potatoes are soft.

Stir the cauliflower mixture, mustard, ketchup and Cheddar cheese into the soup. Serve the soup immediately topped with the green onions.

Keep the soup in the refrigerator for up to 7 days or in the freezer for up to 60 days.

Serving Size: ⅙ **Calories:** 224 **Protein:** 23.9 grams **Carbohydrates:** 24.9 grams **Fiber:** 3.8 grams **Sugar:** 3.8 grams **Fat:** 4.2 grams **Sat. Fat:** 1.1 grams

CALORIES:

132

SLOW COOKER CHICKEN ZOODLE SOUP

This chicken soup recipe has all the flavor of classic chicken soup but it is lightened up using zucchini noodles ("zoodles") instead of traditional noodles. It's an easy soup recipe to make in a slow cooker or pressure cooker for a comforting and nutritious meal!

Serves: 6

4 (4-oz [112-g]) boneless, skinless chicken breasts

1 cup (100 g) diced celery

1 cup (128 g) diced carrots

¼ cup (60 ml) fresh lemon juice

6 cups (1.4 L) low-sodium chicken broth

1 tsp dried thyme

1 tsp dried parsley

3 dried bay leaves

6 cups (900 g) unpeeled spiralized zucchini

In a slow cooker or pressure cooker, combine the chicken, celery, carrots, lemon juice, broth, thyme, parsley and bay leaves. Cover the slow cooker or pressure cooker.

If you are using a slow cooker, cook the soup for 4 hours on high or for 8 hours on low.

If you are using a pressure cooker, set the steam release valve to the sealing position and set the cooker to pressure-cook for 30 minutes. (Note that it will take extra time for the pressure cooker to come to pressure.) After the pressure cooker is done, manually release the pressure.

Remove the cover from the slow cooker or pressure cooker and shred the chicken using two forks. It will shred easily.

Remove and discard the bay leaves. Serve the soup over the spiralized zucchini.

When storing the soup and spiralized zucchini, keep the spiralized zucchini separate from the soup, as it will make it soggy. Store the soup in the refrigerator for up to 7 days or in the freezer for up to 60 days.

Serving Size: ⅙ **Calories:** 132 **Protein:** 38 grams **Carbohydrates:** 6.1 grams **Fiber:** 1.9 grams **Sugar:** 5.9 grams **Fat:** 2.4 grams **Sat. Fat:** 0.1 gram

CREAMY CHICKEN AND WILD RICE SOUP

This hearty wild rice soup is made in a slow cooker with chicken, vegetables and pureed cashews. The cashews give this soup its creamy consistency while boosting the nutrition and adding healthy fat—this is a low-calorie soup with few ingredients and so much flavor!

Serves: 6

⅓ cup (37 g) raw cashews

3 (4-oz [112-g]) boneless, skinless chicken breasts

1 cup (100 g) diced celery

1 cup (128 g) diced carrots

1 tbsp (9 g) minced garlic

2 tsp (2 g) poultry seasoning

1 dried bay leaf

Salt, as needed

Black pepper, as needed

6 cups (1.4 L) low-sodium chicken broth

1 cup (160 g) uncooked wild rice

½ tsp dried parsley

Place the cashews in a small bowl and fill the bowl with enough water to cover the nuts. Set the cashews aside to soak for 1 hour.

In a slow cooker, combine the chicken, celery, carrots, garlic, poultry seasoning, bay leaf, salt, black pepper and broth. Cover the slow cooker and cook the soup for 3 hours on high or for 7 hours on low.

Add the cashews and soaking water to a blender. Blend on high speed until the cashews are creamy. Add more water to the blender if the mixture is too thick to blend. The consistency should be like buttermilk.

Stir the blended cashews into the soup. Add the wild rice and parsley. Cover the slow cooker and cook the soup for an additional 1 hour on high, or until the wild rice is soft.

Before serving, remove and discard the bay leaf, then shred the chicken in the slow cooker using two forks. It will shred easily.

Store the soup in the refrigerator for up to 7 days or in the freezer for up to 60 days.

Serving Size: ⅙ **Calories:** 244 **Protein:** 19.5 grams **Carbohydrates:** 29.6 grams **Fiber:** 2.6 grams **Sugar:** 2.1 grams **Fat:** 5.2 grams **Sat. Fat:** 0.6 gram

THINNER
DINNERS

These dinner recipes are healthier, low-calorie spins on traditional family recipes. All of my dinner recipes are 500 calories or fewer and are made with nutritious, real-food ingredients. Remember, a healthy dinner isn't about a low-calorie number. The quality of the ingredients and the nutritional balance is what's important. A healthy, low-calorie dinner should be one that's high in protein and fiber and that includes a variety of produce and healthy fat. I hope these dinner recipes inspire you to get creative with your own recipes to make them more nutritious!

CALORIES:

367

CAJUN CHICKEN ZUCCHINI NOODLES

This Cajun-spiced chicken recipe is for the pasta lover! The recipe replaces heavy cream with cashews and milk to make a lighter sun-dried tomato and roasted red pepper sauce. It also uses zucchini noodles in place of pasta, making this a kickin' meal that's flavorful and filling!

Serves: 4

½ cup (55 g) raw cashews

2 medium red bell peppers, divided

1 medium green bell pepper

2 tbsp (30 ml) extra-virgin olive oil

12 oz (336 g) boneless, skinless chicken breasts

1 tsp dried oregano

1 tsp garlic powder

1 tsp onion powder

1 tsp paprika

½ tsp cayenne pepper

Salt, as needed

Black pepper, as needed

3 tbsp (45 ml) unsweetened almond milk, low-fat milk or milk of choice

2 tbsp (6 g) finely chopped oil-packed sun-dried tomatoes

4 small zucchini

Soak the cashews in a bowl of water for 30 minutes.

Preheat the oven to 350°F (177°C). Slice 1 red bell pepper in half. Cut off the stem, remove the seeds and place the pepper halves in a small baking dish. Roast the bell pepper for 15 minutes, until it is soft. Remove the baking dish from the oven and let the bell pepper cool in the baking dish while you prepare the other ingredients.

Clean and dice the remaining red bell pepper and green bell pepper into 1-inch (2.5-cm) pieces. In a large skillet over medium heat, combine the red bell pepper, green bell pepper and oil. Cook the bell peppers for 5 to 7 minutes, or until they are soft.

While the bell peppers cook, cut the chicken into 1-inch (2.5-cm) pieces. Add the chicken, oregano, garlic powder, onion powder, paprika, cayenne pepper, salt and black pepper to the skillet. Stir and cook the mixture for 7 to 10 minutes, until the chicken is cooked through.

While the chicken cooks, drain the cashews and discard the water. Transfer the cashews to a blender. Add the milk, roasted red pepper, sun-dried tomatoes and salt. Blend until the ingredients are smooth. Spiralize the zucchini. Add the spiralized zucchini and sauce to the skillet. Toss the spiralized zucchini and sauce with the chicken and bell peppers. Serve.

Store the recipe in the refrigerator for up to 5 days. For meal prepping, leave the spiralized zucchini out of the sauce and store separately. Combine with the sauce when ready to heat and eat.

Serving Size: ¼ **Calories:** 367 **Protein:** 32.5 grams **Carbohydrates:** 18.6 grams **Fiber:** 8.2 grams **Sugar:** 9.9 grams **Fat:** 18.4 grams **Sat. Fat:** 3.3 grams

CALORIES:

302

CHICKEN FRANCESE

This chicken Francese is a pan-fried Italian American chicken dish made with oat flour. Oat flour is a simple ingredient that's low in calories and high in fiber, a great substitute to traditional flours. This easy restaurant-quality recipe is one you can make any day of the week. Serve it in fewer than thirty minutes with your favorite veggies on the side.

Serves: 4

1 lb (450 g) boneless, skinless chicken breasts

¼ cup (23 g) oat flour

1 tsp Italian seasoning

½ tsp salt

2 large eggs

2 tbsp (30 ml) avocado oil

Juice of 1 lemon, plus more as needed

Finely chopped fresh parsley, as needed (optional)

Quartered lemons, as needed (optional)

Cut each chicken breast in half. Place each breast between two pieces of plastic wrap and pound the breast with a mallet until it is ¼ inch (6 mm) thick. Set the chicken breasts aside.

In a medium bowl, combine the oat flour, Italian seasoning and salt. In a second medium bowl, whisk the eggs.

In a large skillet over medium-high heat, combine the oil and lemon juice.

Working in batches, dredge the flattened chicken in the oat mixture and then dredge it in the egg mixture.

Add the coated chicken to the skillet and cook it for 5 minutes on each side, or until it is golden brown and cooked through. Repeat this process with the remaining chicken. Discard any leftover oat flour and egg mixture.

Transfer the cooked chicken to a plate and drizzle it with additional lemon juice. Serve the chicken immediately with the parsley (if using) and lemons (if using).

Serving Size: ¼ **Calories:** 302 **Protein:** 39 grams **Carbohydrates:** 6 grams **Fiber:** 1 gram **Sugar:** 0 grams **Fat:** 14 grams **Sat. Fat:** 2.8 grams

CALORIES:

354

Serves: 4

PARMESAN BAKED SHRIMP SCAMPI AND BROCCOLI RICE

This recipe is a healthier version of shrimp scampi made with less fat, fewer calories and more flavor. Juicy shrimp are topped with oat-Parmesan crumbs and baked until they are golden brown with broccoli rice snuck in between them. This is a warm and filling weeknight casserole for the shrimp lover!

1½ lbs (675 g) medium shrimp, peeled, tails removed and deveined

1 cup (100 g) broccoli rice

¼ cup (60 ml) fresh lemon juice

3 tbsp (45 ml) avocado oil

2 tbsp (19 g) minced shallot

2 tbsp (18 g) minced garlic

Salt, as needed

Black pepper, as needed

⅔ cup (53 g) rolled oats

1 large egg white

¼ cup (45 g) grated Parmesan cheese, plus more as needed

½ tsp red pepper flakes

Finely chopped fresh parsley, as needed (optional)

Quartered lemons, as needed (optional)

Preheat the oven to 425°F (218°C).

In a large bowl, combine the shrimp, broccoli rice, lemon juice, oil, shallot, garlic, salt and black pepper. Stir to combine the ingredients, then transfer the shrimp mixture to a 2-quart (1.9-L) baking dish.

Place the rolled oats in a blender. Pulse just until the oats are broken down and resemble breadcrumbs.

Transfer the oats to a medium bowl. Add the egg white, Parmesan cheese and red pepper flakes. Add just enough water to coat the dry ingredients (about 2 tablespoons [30 ml]), then mix to combine the ingredients. Sprinkle the oat-Parmesan mixture evenly over the shrimp.

Bake the casserole for 12 minutes, then increase the oven's temperature to high broil. Broil the casserole for 2 minutes, until the top is crispy. Remove the casserole from the oven and serve it immediately garnished with the parsley (if using), lemons (if using) and additional Parmesan cheese (if using).

Store the casserole in the refrigerator for up to 3 days.

Serving Size: ¼ **Calories:** 354 **Protein:** 41.5 grams **Carbohydrates:** 16.5 grams **Fiber:** 2.3 grams **Sugar:** 0.7 gram **Fat:** 14.6 grams **Sat. Fat:** 2.3 grams

PESTO EDAMAME SPAGHETTI WITH CHICKEN SAUSAGE

This twenty-minute dinner recipe is a winner with its healthy ingredients. It's made lighter with a homemade oil-free pesto sauce and higher in protein with edamame spaghetti tossed with chicken sausage and grape tomatoes. This is a yummy, low-calorie pesto pasta you can feel good about eating!

Serves: 2

PASTA

4 oz (112 g) edamame spaghetti

2 links precooked nitrate- and sugar-free chicken sausage, thinly sliced

1 cup (150 g) grape tomatoes, sliced in half

PESTO

1 small zucchini

½ cup (20 g) fresh basil leaves

2 tbsp (16 g) walnuts

2 cloves garlic

¼ cup (60 ml) water

2 tbsp (30 ml) fresh lemon juice

½ tsp salt

To make the pasta, bring a medium pot of water to a boil over high heat. Add the edamame spaghetti and cook according to package instructions. Drain the spaghetti and set it aside.

To make the pesto, roughly chop the zucchini, then place it in a food processor or blender. Add the basil leaves, walnuts, garlic, water, lemon juice and salt. Blend on high until the pesto is smooth. Transfer the pesto to a large skillet over medium heat.

Add the chicken sausage, grape tomatoes and spaghetti to the pesto. Toss to combine the ingredients and cook the pasta for 2 to 3 minutes to heat the chicken sausage, then serve.

Serving Size: ½ **Calories:** 466 **Protein:** 39.3 grams **Carbohydrates:** 32.9 grams **Fiber:** 14.1 grams **Sugar:** 13.4 grams **Fat:** 19.5 grams **Sat. Fat:** 4.1 grams

CALORIES:

479

Serves: 4

HEALTHIER HAMBURGER HELPER

This Hamburger Helper recipe is a lighter version of a family meal that adds vegetables to make it a healthier and more filling low-calorie meal. Served with high-protein chickpea pasta, this meal is a better-for-you version of your childhood favorite!

1 tbsp (15 ml) extra-virgin olive oil

1 lb (450 g) 93% lean ground beef or turkey

½ cup (75 g) diced white onion

⅓ cup (43 g) diced carrots

⅓ cup (33 g) diced celery

1 medium red bell pepper, diced

2 tbsp (18 g) minced garlic

8 oz (224 g) chickpea rotini

14 oz (392 g) canned diced tomatoes, undrained

2 cups (480 ml) low-sodium chicken or beef broth

1 tsp dried basil

1 tsp dried oregano

1 tsp salt

½ tsp paprika

½ tsp chili powder

½ tsp black pepper

½ cup (60 g) shredded Cheddar cheese

½ tsp dried parsley

In a large skillet over medium heat, combine the oil, beef, onion, carrots, celery, red bell pepper and garlic. Cook the mixture for 5 minutes, or until the beef has browned, using a wooden spoon to break up the meat while it cooks.

Add the rotini, tomatoes with their juices, broth, basil, oregano, salt, paprika, chili powder and black pepper. Stir the mixture, then cover the skillet with a lid and cook the mixture for 10 minutes, until the liquid has absorbed and the pasta is al dente. Add the Cheddar cheese and parsley, then serve.

Store leftovers in the refrigerator for up to 5 days.

Serving Size: ¼ **Calories:** 479 **Protein:** 37.5 grams **Carbohydrates:** 47.5 grams **Fiber:** 11.1 grams **Sugar:** 10.9 grams **Fat:** 17.7 grams **Sat. Fat:** 6 grams

CALORIES:

228

CHICKEN TACO BAKE

This chicken taco bake is a wholesome, protein-packed dinner with a spicy kick. Made with lean ground chicken and a rainbow of vegetables, it's naturally low-calorie, easy to make for a throw-together meal, freezable and family-approved—all with fewer than 300 calories per serving!

Serves: 6

1 medium sweet potato, peeled and diced

2 tbsp (30 ml) extra-virgin olive oil, divided

Salt, as needed

1 medium red bell pepper, diced

1 medium yellow bell pepper, diced

1 medium green bell pepper, diced

1 small jalapeño, diced

1 lb (450 g) ground chicken

1 tsp onion powder

1 tsp dried oregano

1 tsp ground cumin

½ tsp paprika

½ tsp chili powder

Black pepper, as needed

1 cup (260 g) red salsa

3 large eggs

½ cup (60 g) shredded Cheddar cheese

Diced avocado, as needed (optional)

Coarsely chopped fresh cilantro, as needed (optional)

Cooked brown rice or coarsely chopped lettuce, as needed (optional)

Preheat the oven to 400°F (204°C). Line a medium baking sheet with parchment paper.

Place the sweet potato on the prepared baking sheet and toss it with 1 tablespoon (15 ml) of the oil. Sprinkle the sweet potato with salt. Bake the sweet potato for 15 minutes, until it is tender. Remove the sweet potato from the oven and set it aside. Reduce the oven's temperature to 350°F (177°C).

While the sweet potato bakes, combine the remaining 1 tablespoon (15 ml) of oil, red bell pepper, yellow bell pepper, green bell pepper and jalapeño in a large sauté pan over medium heat. Cook the mixture for 4 minutes, then add the chicken, onion powder, oregano, cumin, paprika, chili powder, salt and black pepper. Cook the mixture for 5 minutes, breaking up the meat with a wooden spoon as it cooks.

In a large bowl, whisk together the salsa, eggs and Cheddar cheese. Stir in the chicken mixture and sweet potato, then transfer the casserole mixture to an 8 x 8-inch (20 x 20–cm) baking dish.

Bake the casserole, uncovered, for 1 hour and 15 minutes, until the center is set.

Remove the casserole from the oven and serve as desired with the avocado (if using) and cilantro (if using) over the brown rice or lettuce (if using).

Store leftovers in the refrigerator for up to 5 days.

Serving Size: ⅙ **Calories:** 228 **Protein:** 20.7 grams **Carbohydrates:** 13.6 grams **Fiber:** 2.5 grams **Sugar:** 6 grams **Fat:** 10.6 grams **Sat. Fat:** 3.5 grams

CALORIES:

248

ASIAN BARBECUE PULLED CHICKEN

Asian flavors meet Southern cusine in a lighter way with this healthier Asian barbecue pulled chicken! This easy, throw-together meal has fewer calories and fat than takeout and uses simple ingredients to make it incredibly delicious.

Serves: 4

1 lb (450 g) boneless, skinless chicken breasts

½ cup (120 ml) barbecue sauce

¼ cup (60 ml) rice wine vinegar

¼ cup (45 g) creamy peanut butter

1 tbsp (15 ml) Sriracha sauce

2 tbsp (30 ml) coconut aminos

2 tbsp (30 ml) fresh lime juice

1 tbsp (9 g) minced ginger

Coarsely chopped fresh cilantro, as needed (optional)

Thinly sliced green onions, as needed (optional)

Salad or brown rice, to serve

To make the chicken in a pressure cooker, place the chicken, barbecue sauce, vinegar, peanut butter, Sriracha sauce, coconut aminos, lime juice and ginger in a pressure cooker. Cover the pressure cooker and set the steam release valve to the sealing position. (Note that it will take extra time for the pressure cooker to come to pressure.) Pressure-cook the mixture for 30 minutes, then use a slow release.

To make the chicken in a slow cooker, place the chicken, barbecue sauce, vinegar, peanut butter, Sriracha sauce, coconut aminos, lime juice and ginger in a slow cooker. Cover the slow cooker and cook the chicken for 4 hours on high or 8 hours on low.

Once the chicken is cooked through, use two forks to shred the chicken. Stir the sauce in with the shredded chicken. Serve the pulled chicken garnished with the cilantro (if using) and green onions (if using) over a salad or brown rice.

Store leftovers in the refrigerator for up to 5 days.

Serving Size: ¼ **Calories:** 248 **Protein:** 29.5 grams **Carbohydrates:** 7.3 grams **Fiber:** 1 gram **Sugar:** 4.2 grams **Fat:** 10.1 grams **Sat. Fat:** 1.7 grams

SKINNY OATMEAL PIZZA CRUST

No more skipping pizza to lose weight! This low-calorie pizza crust combines egg whites, whole-grain oats and milk to make an easy, high-fiber pizza crust that's also delicious. The best part is that it can be made in fewer than ten minutes. Just add your favorite toppings and eat!

Serves: 2

3 large egg whites

1 cup (80 g) rolled oats

¼ cup (60 ml) unsweetened almond milk, low-fat milk or milk of choice

¼ tsp baking powder

¼ tsp salt

Preheat the oven to 375°F (191°C). Line an 18 x 13–inch (45 x 33–cm) baking sheet with parchment paper.

In a blender, combine the egg whites, oats, milk, baking powder and salt. Blend until the ingredients are smooth.

Pour the batter onto the prepared baking sheet. Using a spoon, spread the batter into a circle that is ½ inch (13 mm) thick. The batter will be thin.

Bake the crust for 10 to 12 minutes, until the dough is lightly browned and set up.

Remove the crust from the oven and add your favorite pizza toppings. Bake the pizza for 5 minutes, then remove it from the oven and slice it into four pieces.

Serving Size: ½ **Calories:** 200 **Protein:** 11.5 grams **Carbohydrates:** 33.7 grams **Fiber:** 5.1 grams **Sugar:** 0.3 gram **Fat:** 3.5 grams **Sat. Fat:** 0.5 gram

CALORIES:

322

Serves: 4

SLOW COOKER SESAME BEEF

This dish is lighter than your favorite Chinese takeout. Made easily in a slow cooker, this recipe uses high-quality ingredients, like real honey and coconut aminos, to give the meal full flavor while keeping it light by using less sugar and oil. It's a comforting yet simple recipe.

1 lb (450 g) flank steak or skirt steak

½ cup (120 ml) low-sodium beef broth

2 tbsp (30 ml) coconut aminos

2 tbsp (30 ml) rice wine vinegar

2 tbsp (30 ml) honey

1 tbsp (9 g) minced garlic

1 tbsp (9 g) minced ginger

12 oz (336 g) broccoli florets

2 tbsp (20 g) white sesame seeds

Thinly sliced green onions, as needed (optional)

Cooked brown rice, quinoa or cauliflower rice, as needed (optional)

In a slow cooker, combine the flank steak, broth, coconut aminos, vinegar, honey, garlic and ginger. Cover the slow cooker and cook for 3½ hours on high or for 7 hours on low.

Add the broccoli florets to the slow cooker and cook them for 30 minutes, until they are tender.

Using two forks, shred the steak. Add the sesame seeds and green onions (if using).

Serve the beef and broccoli over the brown rice, quinoa or cauliflower rice (if using) with leftover liquid from the slow cooker.

Store leftovers in the refrigerator for up to 5 days.

Serving Size: ¼ **Calories:** 322 **Protein:** 38.8 grams **Carbohydrates:** 13.4 grams **Fiber:** 1.6 grams **Sugar:** 10.4 grams **Fat:** 13 grams **Sat. Fat:** 4.8 grams

CALORIES:

373

ZUCCHINI AND BEEF ENCHILADA SKILLET

This light and easy beef enchilada comes together in fewer than thirty minutes. Made in a skillet with beans and vegetables that are naturally lower in calories, it makes the perfect Mexican-inspired meal. Just add your favorite enchilada sauce for a flavorful meal with a kick of spice!

Serves: 4

1 lb (450 g) flank steak, diced into 1-inch (2.5-cm) cubes, or 1 lb (450 g) 99% lean ground beef, turkey or chicken

2 tbsp (30 ml) low-sodium beef or chicken broth

Salt, as needed

Black pepper, as needed

1 cup (175 g) diced red bell pepper

1 cup (125 g) diced zucchini

⅓ cup (50 g) diced red onion

2 tbsp (11 g) diced jalapeño

2 tbsp (18 g) minced garlic

1 cup (175 g) frozen corn

1 cup (172 g) canned black beans, drained and rinsed

½ cup (120 ml) red enchilada sauce

½ tsp ground cumin

Diced avocado, as needed (optional)

Coarsely chopped fresh cilantro, as needed (optional)

In a large skillet over medium heat, combine the steak and broth. Season the steak with the salt and black pepper. Cook the steak for 5 minutes, then flip it. Add the bell pepper, zucchini, onion, jalapeño and garlic. Stir to combine and cook the mixture for 5 minutes, until the vegetables are beginning to soften.

Stir in the corn, black beans, enchilada sauce and cumin. Cook the mixture for 5 to 7 minutes, until all the vegetables are soft and the meat is thoroughly cooked.

Serve the enchilada skillet warm topped with the avocado (if using) and cilantro (if using).

Store leftovers in the refrigerator for up to 5 days.

Serving Size: ¼ **Calories:** 373 **Protein:** 43.7 grams **Carbohydrates:** 29.6 grams **Fiber:** 7 grams **Sugar:** 9 grams **Fat:** 11.4 grams **Sat. Fat:** 4.7 grams

CHINESE TURKEY CAULIFLOWER FRIED RICE

This Chinese turkey cauliflower fried rice is a delicious and healthy twist on a classic takeout favorite. Swapping cauliflower rice not only makes this dish lower in calories but also more filling and nutritious. This recipe is so delicious, you'll never know it's good for you!

Serves: 4

1 lb (450 g) 99% lean ground turkey or chicken

1 tbsp (15 ml) extra-virgin olive oil

¼ cup (38 g) yellow onion, diced

1 cup (50 g) shredded carrots

½ tbsp (8 ml) chili-garlic sauce

1 tbsp (9 g) minced garlic

½ tbsp (5 g) ground ginger

1 tsp Sriracha sauce

¼ cup (60 ml) coconut aminos or soy sauce

2 tbsp (30 ml) rice wine vinegar

2 large eggs

12 oz (336 g) cauliflower rice

½ cup (75 g) frozen baby peas

4 tbsp (8 g) finely chopped green onions

In a large skillet over medium heat, combine the turkey, oil, onion and carrots. Cook the mixture for 5 to 7 minutes, breaking up the meat with a wooden spoon as it cooks.

Add the chili-garlic sauce, garlic, ginger, Sriracha sauce, coconut aminos and vinegar. Stir to combine and cook the mixture for 3 minutes, continuing to break up the meat with a wooden spoon.

Whisk the eggs together in a small bowl, then add them to a small skillet over medium heat. Cook the eggs for 4 minutes on one side, then flip them like a pancake and cook them for 4 minutes on the other side.

Transfer the eggs to a cutting board and roughly chop them into 1-inch (2.5-cm) pieces.

Stir the cauliflower rice, peas and eggs into the turkey and vegetable mixture. Cook the mixture for 5 minutes, then serve the fried cauliflower rice immediately topped with the green onions.

Store leftovers in the refrigerator for up to 5 days.

Serving Size: ¼ **Calories:** 235 **Protein:** 31.3 grams **Carbohydrates:** 10.2 grams **Fiber:** 3.1 grams **Sugar:** 4.1 grams **Fat:** 8 grams **Sat. Fat:** 1.8 grams

CALORIES:

374

BAKED FISH 'N' CHIPS

This easy recipe is a quick and healthy version of traditional fried fish and chips that bakes in the oven on a baking sheet. The fish is breaded in almond flour, which is a healthier alternative to traditional flours and makes the perfect crispy crust on the outside while keeping the fish tender on the inside. This is a hearty low-calorie meal that's balanced in nutrition!

Serves: 4

1 lb (450 g) frozen cod fillets, thawed

1 cup (96 g) almond flour

¼ cup (31 g) arrowroot starch or tapioca flour

1 tsp paprika

½ tsp garlic powder

½ tsp black pepper

¼ tsp cayenne pepper

¼ tsp salt, plus more as needed

1 large egg white

2 tbsp (30 ml) water

2 medium russet potatoes

Avocado oil spray

Preheat the oven to 425°F (218°C). Line two large baking sheets with parchment paper. Place the cod on a plate and pat dry with a paper towel.

In a medium bowl, stir together the flour, arrowroot starch, paprika, garlic powder, black pepper, cayenne pepper and salt.

In another medium bowl, whisk together the egg white and water. Whisk together until bubbles form, then set the bowl aside.

Scrub the potatoes, then cut them diagonally into 1-inch (2.5-cm)-thick slices. Place them on one of the prepared baking sheets. Spray the potatoes with the avocado oil spray and sprinkle them with the additional salt. Bake the potatoes for 20 minutes while you prepare the cod.

Dip one cod fillet into the egg wash, then immediately into the flour mixture, using your hands to cover the cod thoroughly with the breading. Transfer the cod to the second prepared baking sheet and repeat the process for the remaining cod. Discard any leftover flour mixture or egg mixture.

Place the cod in the oven and flip the fries. Reduce the oven's temperature to 375°F (191°C). Bake the fries for another 20 minutes and the cod for 30 minutes, until both are golden brown. Remove the fries and cod from the oven and serve.

Store leftovers in the refrigerator for up to 3 days. Reheat leftovers in an oven preheated to 350°F (177°C) for 20 minutes.

Serving Size: ¼ **Calories:** 374 **Protein:** 33.5 grams **Carbohydrates:** 28.2 grams **Fiber:** 6 grams **Sugar:** 2 grams **Fat:** 15.2 grams **Sat. Fat:** 1.2 grams

CALORIES:

375

Serves: 3

PIZZA CHICKEN

If you love pizza, you'll love this pizza-flavored chicken bake. This meal has all the flavor of pizza with fewer calories, because it uses turkey pepperoni, less cheese and a sugar-free pizza sauce. It's a high-protein meal that doesn't taste healthy!

3 (4-oz [112-g]) boneless, skinless chicken breasts

1¾ cups (420 ml) sugar-free pizza sauce

14 oz (392 g) canned diced tomatoes, drained

½ tsp onion powder

½ tsp garlic powder

½ tsp dried basil

½ tsp salt

½ tsp black pepper

9 slices turkey pepperoni

3 tbsp (15 g) shredded low-moisture mozzarella cheese

Preheat the oven to 400°F (204°C). Place the chicken breasts in a 9 x 13-inch (23 x 33-cm) baking dish.

In a medium bowl, mix together the pizza sauce, tomatoes, onion powder, garlic powder, basil, salt and black pepper. Pour the sauce over the chicken breasts.

Bake the chicken breasts, uncovered, for 50 minutes. Remove them from the oven, add the turkey pepperoni and cheese, then bake the chicken for 5 minutes, until the cheese is melted and the pepperoni is crispy. Remove the chicken from the oven and serve it with the sauce spooned over it.

Store leftovers in the refrigerator for up to 5 days.

Serving Size: ⅓ Calories: 375 Protein: 45.3 grams Carbohydrates: 20 grams Fiber: 4.7 grams Sugar: 9.9 grams Fat: 12.9 grams Sat. Fat: 1.7 grams

CALORIES:

286

Serves: 4

LIGHTER SWEDISH MEATBALLS

This recipe for lighter Swedish meatballs and gravy uses lean ground beef and is cooked in a skillet without oil, making it lower in calories than traditional Swedish meatballs. It's a flavorful recipe that's family-approved and freezable too!

MEATBALLS

¼ cup (20 g) rolled oats

Olive oil spray

¼ cup (38 g) diced white onion

¼ cup (25 g) diced celery

1 lb (450 g) 99% lean ground beef

3 tbsp (45 ml) canned light coconut milk (see note)

2 tbsp (30 ml) coconut aminos or soy sauce

¼ tsp ground nutmeg

½ tsp salt

½ tsp black pepper

2 tsp (2 g) dried parsley, divided

GRAVY

1 tbsp (9 g) cornstarch or arrowroot starch

2 cups (480 ml) low-sodium beef broth

½ cup (120 ml) canned light coconut milk

1 tsp coconut aminos or soy sauce

1 tsp spicy brown mustard

NOTE

Do not swap the coconut milk for another milk, as this is a key ingredient for thickening the sauce.

To make the meatballs, place the oats in a blender. Blend on high for 2 minutes, until the oats form a flour. Set the oat flour aside.

Spray a large skillet with the olive oil spray and set the skillet over medium heat. Add the onion and celery. Cook the vegetables for 2 to 3 minutes, until the onion is translucent.

While the onion and celery cook, place the beef, oats, coconut milk, coconut aminos, nutmeg, salt, black pepper and 1 teaspoon of the parsley in a large bowl. Add the onion and celery to the beef mixture and mix the ingredients together with your hands. Roll the meat mixture into 16 (1½-inch [4-cm]) balls.

Place the skillet over medium heat. Add the meatballs to the skillet and cook them for 7 minutes. Gently flip them over and cook them for another 7 minutes. Once the meatballs have browned, transfer them to a plate. Set the plate aside.

To make the gravy, add the cornstarch to the skillet and whisk it together with the leftover fat from the meat until the mixture is bubbly, 2 to 3 minutes. Add the broth, coconut milk, coconut aminos and mustard. Increase the heat to medium-high and simmer the gravy for 5 minutes to thicken it. Add the meatballs to the skillet and sprinkle with the remaining 1 teaspoon of parsley. Serve the meatballs immediately topped with the gravy.

Store leftovers in the refrigerator for up to 5 days or in the freezer for up to 30 days.

Serving Size: ¼ **Calories:** 286 **Protein:** 24.5 grams **Carbohydrates:** 13.5 grams **Fiber:** 1.5 grams **Sugar:** 1.9 grams **Fat:** 13.8 grams **Sat. Fat:** 6.2 grams

ZOODLES AND VEGGIE CHICKEN MEATBALLS

Zucchini noodles are the perfect low-calorie substitute to flour-based pastas. This recipe pairs zoodles with juicy oven-baked chicken meatballs—it's a veggie-packed meal perfect for picky and healthy eaters alike.

Serves: 4

2 tbsp (30 ml) extra-virgin olive oil

⅓ cup (58 g) diced red bell pepper

½ cup (75 g) shredded zucchini

1 lb (450 g) ground chicken

1 large egg

2 tbsp (12 g) almond flour

½ tsp garlic powder

½ tsp dried parsley

½ tsp salt, plus more as needed

½ tsp black pepper, plus more as needed

½ cup (75 g) diced white onion

½ cup (25 g) shredded carrots

3 cloves garlic, diced

28 oz (784 g) crushed tomatoes, undrained

1 tbsp (3 g) Italian seasoning

4 small zucchini

Preheat the oven to 350°F (177°C). Line a large baking sheet with parchment paper.

In a large skillet over medium heat, combine the oil and red bell pepper. Cook the bell pepper for 5 minutes, until it is slightly tender, then add the shredded zucchini. Cook the vegetables for 2 minutes, then transfer them to a large bowl to cool until you can safely handle them. Add the chicken, egg, flour, garlic powder, parsley, ½ teaspoon salt and ½ teaspoon black pepper to the vegetable mixture. Mix everything together with your hands, then roll the mixture into 16 meatballs and place them on the prepared baking sheet. Bake the meatballs for 15 minutes, then flip them and bake them for 12 minutes, or until they are cooked through.

Place the skillet over medium heat. Add the onion, carrots and garlic and cook them for 5 minutes, until they are soft. Add the tomatoes and their juices, Italian seasoning and salt and black pepper as needed. Bring the sauce to a strong simmer, then reduce the heat to low and let the sauce simmer while the meatballs bake.

When the meatballs are finished, increase the oven's temperature to a high broil. Broil the meatballs for 3 minutes to make them crispy on the outside. Watch them carefully so they do not overcook. Remove the meatballs from the oven and remove the sauce from the stove.

Spiralize the zucchinis and divide the zucchini noodles among four plates. Place the meatballs and sauce over the zucchini noodles. Store leftover meatballs in the refrigerator for up to 5 days. For meal prepping, store the zucchini noodles separate from the meatballs and sauce.

Serving Size: ¼ **Calories:** 448 **Protein:** 31.9 grams **Carbohydrates:** 33.6 grams **Fiber:** 8.4 grams **Sugar:** 21.4 grams **Fat:** 21 grams **Sat. Fat:** 4.8 grams

CALORIES:

298

SKINNY MAC 'N' CHEESE

This homemade mac 'n' cheese is lighter and healthier than its traditional counterpart. It has a delicious cauliflower base that replaces heavy cream and cheese. Made with broccoli and high-protein chickpea pasta, this simple recipe is a great way to sneak veggies and plant-based protein into your favorite childhood comfort food!

Serves: 4

4 cups (428 g) cauliflower florets

1 cup (240 ml) water

½ cup (120 ml) low-sodium chicken broth

8 oz (224 g) chickpea pasta

1 tsp salt

1 tsp black pepper

1 cup (240 ml) unsweetened almond milk, low-fat milk or milk of choice

½ cup (60 g) shredded low-moisture Cheddar cheese

2 cups (350 g) broccoli florets

⅓ cup (27 g) rolled oats

In a large pot over high heat, combine the cauliflower and water and bring the water to a boil. Boil for 5 minutes, or until the cauliflower is soft. Drain the cauliflower, then place it in a blender. Add the broth. Blend until the cauliflower is smooth.

Fill the pot with water, place it over high heat and bring the water to a boil. Add the pasta and boil it according to package directions, until it is al dente. Drain the pasta and set it aside.

Preheat the broiler to high.

Add the blended cauliflower, salt, black pepper and milk to the pot. Set the pot over medium-high heat and bring the mixture to a simmer. Cook it for 5 minutes to thicken it. Stir in the pasta, Cheddar cheese and broccoli. Cook for another 5 minutes.

Transfer the mixture to a 9 x 13–inch (23 x 33–cm) baking dish.

Pulse the oats in a blender several times until they resemble breadcrumbs. Sprinkle the crumbs over the pasta, then place the baking dish under the broiler for 5 minutes. Remove the mac 'n' cheese from the oven and serve.

Store in the refrigerator for up to 5 days.

Serving Size: ¼ **Calories:** 298 **Protein:** 21.5 grams **Carbohydrates:** 46 grams **Fiber:** 4.6 grams **Sugar:** 3.5 grams **Fat:** 5.9 grams **Sat. Fat:** 0.8 gram

SPAGHETTI SQUASH SHRIMP FRA DIAVOLO

This dish combines baked shrimp with a spicy tomato sauce served over spaghetti squash. Spaghetti squash is naturally low in calories and more nutritious than flour-based pastas. The sauce is packed with veggies and spices, keeping it lighter than traditional sauces.

Serves: 4

1 medium spaghetti squash (see note)

Avocado oil spray

½ tsp black pepper, plus more as needed, divided

¼ tsp salt, plus more as needed, divided

2 tbsp (30 ml) extra-virgin olive oil

3 cloves garlic, diced

¼ cup (38 g) diced shallot

1 tsp red pepper flakes

¼ cup (60 ml) low-sodium chicken broth

28 oz (784 g) canned crushed tomatoes

½ tsp dried basil

½ tsp dried oregano

1 lb (450 g) frozen shrimp, thawed, tails removed and deveined

¼ cup (45 g) grated Parmesan cheese

¼ cup (15 g) coarsely chopped fresh parsley

Preheat the oven to 400°F (204°C). Line a medium baking sheet with parchment paper.

Slice the spaghetti squash in half lengthwise and use a spoon to remove the seeds. Spray the flesh lightly with the avocado oil spray and season it as needed with the salt and black pepper. Place the squash on the baking sheet flesh-side down. Cover the squash with foil and bake it for 40 to 45 minutes.

In a large skillet over medium heat, combine the oil, garlic, shallot and red pepper flakes. Cook the mixture for 4 minutes, or until the shallot is translucent and the red pepper flakes are fragrant. Stir in the broth, scraping up the remnants on the bottom of the skillet. Add the tomatoes, basil, oregano, remaining ½ teaspoon of black pepper and ¼ teaspoon of salt and bring the sauce to a simmer. Add the shrimp, cover the skillet and cook the shrimp for 5 minutes, or until they are opaque.

Remove the spaghetti squash from the oven and flip it over to cool. Increase the oven's temperature to a high broil. While the broiler preheats, remove the spaghetti squash's flesh from its skin with a fork. Place the flesh in a large bowl, pour the shrimp mixture over it, toss to combine and spoon the mixture back into the empty spaghetti squash.

Sprinkle the Parmesan cheese evenly over the spaghetti squash, then place the squash under the broiler for 3 minutes to melt the cheese. Serve the squash immediately topped with the parsley. Store leftovers in the refrigerator for up to 5 days.

NOTE

If you prefer to use precooked spaghetti squash, you will need 4 cups (620 g).

Serving Size: ¼ **Calories:** 322 **Protein:** 30.7 grams **Carbohydrates:** 27.8 grams **Fiber:** 5.4 grams **Sugar:** 13.5 grams **Fat:** 9.9 grams **Sat. Fat:** 2 grams

SWEET TREATS

Yes, you can enjoy sweet treats on a low-calorie diet! A common misconception about healthy eating is that you have to be restrictive with what you eat. As I mentioned at the beginning of this book, restricting often leads to unhealthy behaviors with food and binge eating. A healthy diet should include the occasional sweet treat that is high-protein, high-fiber and includes healthy fats to balance out the sugar and carbs.

My personal favorites in this chapter are the Peanut Butter Crunch Bites (page 129), Fudgy Black Bean Brownies (page 134) and Chickpea Chocolate Chip Cookies (page 149). Enjoy the yummy goodies!

CALORIES:

118

Serves: 16

PEANUT BUTTER CRUNCH BITES

These yummy bites are your favorite candy bar turned into a healthy snack! You'll love these healthy, no-bake treats that are made with simple, wholesome ingredients and that are only a little over 100 calories each.

¾ cup (60 g) rolled oats

¾ cup (132 g) creamy unsalted, sugar-free peanut butter

¼ cup (60 ml) pure maple syrup

⅓ cup (7 g) puffed rice cereal

¼ cup (44 g) chocolate chips

1 tsp coconut oil

Place the oats in a blender. Blend 1 to 2 minutes until the oats form a flour. Transfer the oat flour to a medium bowl. Add the peanut butter and maple syrup. Stir the ingredients together. The mixture will be thick, but it will come together. Fold the cereal into the peanut butter mixture.

Cover a plate with parchment paper. Use a tablespoon to drop portions of the mixture onto the parchment paper, then use your hands to roll the portions into balls. Refrigerate the balls for 30 minutes.

Place the chocolate and coconut oil in a microwave-safe ramekin and microwave them for 1 to 2 minutes, until they are melted. Remove the plate of bites from the refrigerator and, using a spoon, drizzle the chocolate over the bites. Refrigerate them for another 10 minutes to allow the chocolate to set before serving.

Store the bites in the refrigerator for up to 15 days or in the freezer for up to 90 days.

Serving Size: ⅟₁₆ **Calories:** 118 **Protein:** 4 grams **Carbohydrates:** 10.9 grams **Fiber:** 1.5 grams **Sugar:** 2.5 grams **Fat:** 7.3 grams **Sat. Fat:** 2 grams

TAHINI, VANILLA AND ESPRESSO CHOCOLATE BITES

These tahini, vanilla and espresso chocolate bites are super easy to make and require no baking. Made with healthy fats, protein and rolled oats, these nutritionally balanced snacks are kid-friendly and only 123 calories each.

Serves: 18

1¼ cups (100 g) rolled oats

¼ cup (44 g) vanilla protein powder (see notes)

2 tbsp (14 g) unsweetened cocoa powder

2 tbsp (20 g) chia seeds

1 tsp espresso powder

¼ cup (44 g) mini chocolate chips

¾ cup (180 g) tahini or nut butter (see notes)

¼ cup (60 ml) honey

½ tsp almond or vanilla extract (see notes)

1 to 2 tbsp (15 to 30 ml) unsweetened almond milk, low-fat milk or milk of choice (optional)

In a large bowl, combine the oats, protein powder, cocoa powder, chia seeds, espresso powder and chocolate chips.

Add the tahini, honey and almond extract to the oat mixture and stir to combine. If the mixture is dry and loose, add the milk as needed.

Dampen your hands with water, then scoop out 1 tablespoon (15 g) of the mixture and roll it into a ball with your hands. Place the ball on a plate and repeat this process for the remaining mixture, dampening your hands between rolling the balls. The dampness will keep the balls together.

Refrigerate the bites for 30 minutes, then serve. The bites can be kept in the refrigerator for up to 14 days or in the freezer for up to 60 days.

NOTES

Use a low-carb protein powder with no added sugar. My favorite brands are Garden of Life, Vega Clean and Orgain. The nutrition stats for this recipe are based on Garden of Life.

Use creamy unsalted, sugar-free peanut, almond or cashew butter.

While you may use pure vanilla extract, the almond extract enhances the chocolate flavor.

Serving Size: ⅟₁₈ **Calories:** 123 **Protein:** 3.6 grams **Carbohydrates:** 13.7 grams **Fiber:** 1.9 grams **Sugar:** 5.6 grams **Fat:** 7.1 grams **Sat. Fat:** 1.4 grams

NO-BAKE COOKIE DOUGH

These five-ingredient, no-bake protein bars make a fantastic high-protein, high-fiber snack. They are as healthy as they are delicious!

½ cup (40 g) rolled oats

1 cup (176 g) creamy unsalted, sugar-free peanut butter (see notes)

⅔ cup (117 g) vanilla protein powder (see notes)

2 tbsp (30 ml) pure maple syrup

¼ cup (44 g) chocolate chips

Line a 9 x 5–inch (23 x 13–cm) loaf pan with parchment paper.

Add the oats to a blender and blend for 2 to 3 minutes, until the oats form a flour.

Transfer the oat flour to a medium bowl. Add the peanut butter, protein powder and maple syrup. Stir to combine. It will take a few minutes to combine the dry ingredients with the wet ingredients.

Transfer the dough to the prepared loaf pan and spread the dough into an even layer with your hands. (Damp hands will help with this step.)

Scatter the chocolate chips on top of the dough and press them slightly into it. Place the loaf pan in the refrigerator for 1 hour to allow the cookie dough to set. Remove the cookie dough from the refrigerator and slice it into five bars.

Store the protein bars in the refrigerator until you are ready to serve. The bars will keep for up to 10 days in the refrigerator and in the freezer for up to 60 days.

NOTES

If you prefer, you can use almond, cashew or sunflower butter instead of peanut butter.

Use a low-carb protein powder with no added sugar. My favorite brands are Garden of Life, Vega Clean and Orgain. The nutrition stats for this recipe are based on Garden of Life.

Serving Size: ⅕ **Calories:** 169 **Protein:** 11.4 grams **Carbohydrates:** 20.7 grams **Fiber:** 2.9 grams **Sugar:** 9.6 grams **Fat:** 5.7 grams **Sat. Fat:** 1.9 grams

FUDGY BLACK BEAN BROWNIES

Black beans replace flour in these brownies, making them super fudgy while lower in calories. These brownies are packed with fiber and protein—but no one will ever know these decadent brownies are made with beans!

Serves: 8

1 (15-oz [420-g]) can low-sodium black beans, drained and rinsed

3 tbsp (46 g) coconut oil, melted, divided

3 large eggs

1 tsp pure vanilla extract

¼ cup (28 g) unsweetened cocoa powder

⅓ cup (64 g) coconut sugar

½ tsp baking powder

¼ tsp salt

½ tsp espresso powder

⅓ cup (60 g) chocolate chips, divided

Preheat the oven to 350°F (177°C). Line a 9 x 5–inch (23 x 13–cm) loaf pan with parchment paper.

Place the beans and 1½ tablespoons (23 g) of the coconut oil in a food processor or blender. Process until the beans are pureed and have formed a coarse paste.

Transfer the black bean paste to a large bowl. Add the eggs and vanilla. Stir the ingredients together until they are smooth. Add the cocoa powder, sugar, baking powder, remaining 1½ tablespoons (23 g) of coconut oil, salt and espresso powder. Stir to combine. Fold half (30 g) of the chocolate chips into the batter.

Transfer the batter to the prepared loaf pan and smooth the batter into an even layer. Scatter the remaining half (30 g) of the chocolate chips on top of the batter.

Bake the brownies for 30 minutes, or until the top is set. Remove the brownies from the oven and let them cool in the loaf pan for 30 minutes before slicing and serving.

Serving Size: ⅛ **Calories:** 188 **Protein:** 6 grams **Carbohydrates:** 22.2 grams **Fiber:** 5.3 grams **Sugar:** 10.4 grams **Fat:** 9.2 grams **Sat. Fat:** 6.3 grams

CARROT–PEANUT BUTTER BLONDIES

These rich, fudgy blondies are made flourless and egg-free with peanut butter, maple syrup and carrots. The ingredients are nutritionally balanced so the blondies are higher in protein and fiber while being low in calories. They are a healthier way to get your chocolate fix!

Serves: 9

2 tbsp (14 g) flax meal

¼ cup (60 ml) water

1 cup (50 g) shredded carrots

¾ cup (132 g) creamy unsalted, sugar-free peanut butter

¼ cup (60 ml) pure maple syrup

1 tbsp (15 ml) pure vanilla extract

½ tsp baking soda

¼ tsp salt

4 tbsp (44 g) chocolate chips, divided

Preheat the oven to 350°F (177°C). Line an 8 x 8-inch (20 x 20-cm) baking pan with parchment paper.

In a small bowl, stir together the flax meal and water. Set the mixture aside to thicken for 3 to 4 minutes.

Add the carrots to a blender and pulse several times until they are finely chopped. Transfer the carrots to a large bowl. Add the flax mixture, peanut butter, maple syrup, vanilla, baking soda and salt.

Fold 3½ tablespoons (39 g) of the chocolate chips into the batter. Transfer the batter to the prepared baking dish and smooth the batter into an even layer. Add the remaining ½ tablespoon (5 g) of the chocolate chips on top of the batter.

Bake the blondies for 25 minutes. Remove the blondies from the oven and let them cool completely, about 1 hour, before slicing them into nine pieces.

Store the blondies in the refrigerator for up to 12 days.

Serving Size: ⅑ **Calories:** 187 **Protein:** 6 grams **Carbohydrates:** 14.8 grams **Fiber:** 2.3 grams **Sugar:** 10.5 grams **Fat:** 12.6 grams **Sat. Fat:** 3.1 grams

DOUBLE CHOCOLATE ZUCCHINI BREAD

This double chocolate zucchini bread is made with nutrient-dense almond flour, a better option than traditional flours for balancing blood sugar. The zucchini makes this recipe lower in calories by replacing a large portion of oil. This is a zucchini bread with all the rich, moist flavor and fewer calories!

Serves: 12

2⅛ cups (204 g) almond flour

¼ cup (28 g) plus 2 tbsp (14 g) unsweetened cocoa powder

¾ tsp baking soda

½ tsp salt

⅓ cup (80 ml) pure maple syrup

3 tbsp (45 g) coconut oil

½ tsp pure vanilla extract

3 large eggs

1½ cups (225 g) shredded zucchini

¼ cup (44 g) mini chocolate chips

Preheat the oven to 350°F (177°C). Line a 9 x 5–inch (23 x 13–cm) baking pan with parchment paper.

In a large bowl, stir together the flour, cocoa powder, baking soda and salt. Set the bowl aside.

In a food processor, combine the maple syrup, coconut oil, vanilla and eggs and process until the ingredients are smooth. Add the flour mixture and process again to combine. The mixture will be watery.

Pour the mixture into the bowl that had contained the flour mixture. Fold in the zucchini and chocolate chips, reserving a few chocolate chips for the top of the loaf. Transfer the mixture into the prepared baking pan and sprinkle reserved chocolate chips on top.

Bake the zucchini bread for 50 to 55 minutes, or until a toothpick inserted into the center comes out clean.

Remove the zucchini bread from the oven and let it cool for 1 hour in the baking pan before removing it from the pan and slicing it.

Store leftover bread in the refrigerator for up to 7 days or in the freezer for up to 30 days.

Serving Size: ½ **Calories:** 219 **Protein:** 6.5 grams **Carbohydrates:** 15.8 grams **Fiber:** 4.1 grams **Sugar:** 9.4 grams **Fat:** 16.2 grams **Sat. Fat:** 4.9 grams

SINGLE-SERVE CHOCOLATE CHIP COOKIE DOUGH

Cookie dough that's good for you? Yes! This cookie dough is high in fiber from whole-grain oats and uses applesauce to keep the sugar content lower than traditional cookie dough desserts. It's a low-calorie treat perfectly portioned in a ramekin for single serving.

Serves: 1

Avocado oil spray

3 tbsp (45 g) unsweetened applesauce

½ tbsp (8 ml) pure maple syrup

½ tbsp (6 g) creamy unsalted, sugar-free peanut butter

¼ cup (23 g) oat flour (see note)

½ tsp baking powder

¼ tsp salt

½ tbsp (6 g) mini chocolate chips

Spray a microwave-safe ramekin with the avocado oil spray.

In a medium bowl, stir together the applesauce, maple syrup and peanut butter. Set the bowl aside.

In another medium bowl, combine the flour, baking powder and salt.

Add the flour mixture to the applesauce mixture. Gently fold to combine. Do not overmix.

Transfer the batter to the prepared ramekin. Top the batter with the chocolate chips.

Microwave the cookie dough for 2 minutes, or until the batter has risen and a toothpick inserted into the center comes out clean.

Serve the cookie dough immediately or store it in the refrigerator, covered, for up to 7 days. Reheat it in the microwave for 60 seconds to eat.

NOTE

If you are making your own oat flour, place ¼ cup (20 g) of rolled oats in a blender and blend them for 2 minutes, until the oats form a flour.

Serving Size: 1 **Calories:** 214 **Protein:** 5.1 grams **Carbohydrates:** 35.6 grams **Fiber:** 3.5 grams **Sugar:** 15 grams **Fat:** 7.6 grams **Sat. Fat:** 2.3 grams

SINGLE-SERVE DOUBLE CHOCOLATE COOKIE

This single-serve cookie is perfect for when you want a healthy treat. Made high-fiber with coconut flour, this cookie not only fills you up but also makes a guiltless low-calorie treat. The best part: no baking required!

Serves: 1

Avocado oil spray

1 large egg

¼ cup (60 ml) unsweetened almond milk or low-fat milk

1 tbsp (15 ml) pure maple syrup

2 tbsp (14 g) coconut flour (see note)

1 tbsp (7 g) unsweetened cocoa powder

¼ tsp baking powder

¼ tsp salt

1 tbsp (11 g) mini chocolate chips

Spray a microwave-safe ramekin with the avocado oil spray.

In a medium bowl, whisk together the egg, milk and maple syrup. Set the bowl aside.

In another medium bowl, combine the flour, cocoa powder, baking powder and salt.

Add the flour mixture to the egg mixture. Gently fold to combine. Do not overmix, as coconut flour is very absorbent.

Transfer the batter to the prepared ramekin. Top the batter with the chocolate chips.

Microwave the cookie for 2 minutes, or until the batter has risen and a toothpick inserted into the center comes out clean.

Serve the cookie immediately or store it in the refrigerator, covered, for up to 7 days. Reheat it in the microwave for 60 seconds to eat.

NOTE
Do not substitute another flour for the coconut flour in this recipe.

Serving Size: 1 **Calories:** 283 **Protein:** 10 grams **Carbohydrates:** 29.6 grams **Fiber:** 2.3 grams **Sugar:** 20.1 grams **Fat:** 11.9 grams **Sat. Fat:** 4.1 grams

CALORIES:

337

Serves: 1

SINGLE-SERVE CARROT CAKE

Treat yourself to a yummy, low-calorie carrot cake made for one! Made with 12 grams of protein and high-fiber almond and coconut flours, this lightly sweetened treat is a dessert you can feel good about eating and only takes 2 minutes to bake in a microwave.

Avocado oil spray

1 large egg

1 tbsp (15 ml) pure maple syrup

1 tbsp (15 ml) low-fat milk or milk of choice

1 tsp pure vanilla extract

3 tbsp (18 g) almond flour

1 tbsp (7 g) coconut flour (see note)

½ tsp baking powder

½ tsp ground cinnamon, plus more as needed

¼ tsp ground ginger

¼ tsp salt

2 tbsp (6 g) finely shredded carrots

1 tsp melted coconut oil

Shredded coconut flakes, as needed

Spray a microwave-safe ramekin with the avocado oil spray.

In a medium bowl, whisk together the egg, maple syrup, milk and vanilla.

Add the almond flour, coconut flour, baking powder, cinnamon, ginger and salt. Fold to combine the ingredients. Add the carrots and coconut oil to the bowl and stir.

Transfer the batter to the prepared ramekin and microwave it for 2 to 2½ minutes, or until the cake is cooked through and a toothpick inserted into the center comes out clean. Serve the cake with extra cinnamon and a sprinkle of shredded coconut flakes on top.

Serve the cake immediately or store it in the refrigerator, covered, for up to 7 days. Reheat it in the microwave for 60 seconds.

NOTE

Do not substitute another flour for the coconut flour in this recipe.

Serving Size: 1 Calories: 337 Protein: 12 grams Carbohydrates: 23.5 grams Fiber: 4.6 grams Sugar: 13.5 grams Fat: 21.1 grams Sat. Fat: 6.3 grams

CALORIES:

133

Serves: 16

OATMEAL RAISIN COOKIES

Get ready for soft and chewy oatmeal raisin cookies that are lower in sugar and only 133 calories each! They're made with a mix of whole-grain oats, almond flour, coconut sugar and molasses. High-fiber and balanced in healthy fat and protein, these cookies will become your new favorite treat.

2 large eggs

2 tsp (10 ml) pure vanilla extract

2 tbsp (30 ml) molasses

½ cup (96 g) coconut sugar

1 tsp ground cinnamon

2 cups (160 g) rolled oats

2 cups (192 g) almond flour

1 tsp baking soda

½ cup (75 g) seedless raisins (see note)

Preheat the oven to 350°F (177°C). Line two large baking sheets with parchment paper.

In a large bowl, whisk together the eggs, vanilla, molasses, sugar and cinnamon. Fold in the oats, flour and baking soda until the ingredients are combined. (The mixture will be sticky.) Add the raisins and fold them into the batter.

Drop 2 tablespoons (30 g) of the batter onto one of the prepared baking sheets and use your hands to flatten the batter slightly to form a cookie. Repeat this process for the remaining batter and baking sheet until you have 16 cookies. The cookies will spread a lot, so keep them 2 to 3 inches (5 to 7.5 cm) apart on the baking sheets.

Bake the cookies for 8 to 10 minutes, then remove them from the oven and let them cool on the baking sheets for 10 minutes before transferring them to a wire baking rack.

Store leftover cookies in the refrigerator for up to 10 days or in the freezer for up to 60 days.

NOTE

If your raisins are hard, soak them in water for 30 minutes, then pat them dry with a towel before adding to the batter.

Serving Size: ⅟₁₆ **Calories:** 133 **Protein:** 3.9 grams **Carbohydrates:** 14 grams **Fiber:** 2.3 grams **Sugar:** 9.9 grams **Fat:** 7.6 grams **Sat. Fat:** 0.7 gram

CHICKPEA CHOCOLATE CHIP COOKIES

Sink your teeth into these decadent chickpea chocolate chip cookies! They're lower in calories because we're swapping traditional flour with chickpeas. The chickpeas are blended with peanut butter to make a high-protein, high-fiber cookie that's a healthier, low-calorie treat.

1 (14-oz [392-g]) can chickpeas (garbanzo beans), drained and rinsed

1 cup (176 g) creamy unsalted, sugar-free peanut butter

½ cup (120 ml) pure maple syrup

2 tsp (10 ml) pure vanilla extract

1½ tsp (6 g) baking soda

½ tsp salt

½ cup (88 g) mini chocolate chips

Preheat the oven to 350°F (177°C). Line two large baking sheets with parchment paper.

Add the chickpeas to a food processor or blender. Process until the chickpeas are smooth. Add the peanut butter, maple syrup, vanilla, baking soda and salt. Blend again until everything is thoroughly combined. Transfer the dough to a large bowl and fold in the chocolate chips.

Drop 2 tablespoons (30 g) of the dough onto one of the prepared baking sheets and use damp hands to shape the dough into a cookie. The batter will be very sticky—keep your hands damp as you work. Repeat the process with the remaining dough and baking sheet until you have 16 cookies.

Bake the cookies for 15 to 18 minutes. Remove the cookies from the oven and let cool on the baking sheet for 20 minutes before transferring them to a wire baking rack.

Store leftover cookies in the refrigerator for up to 10 days or in the freezer for up to 60 days.

Serving Size: 1/16 **Calories:** 183 **Protein:** 5.3 grams **Carbohydrates:** 19.2 grams **Fiber:** 2.3 grams **Sugar:** 11.7 grams **Fat:** 10.3 grams **Sat. Fat:** 2.9 grams

CALORIES:

125

MORNING GLORY MUFFINS

These morning glory muffins are made with almond flour. The healthy fat makes them more filling than muffins made from traditional flour. They're lightly sweetened with real maple syrup and applesauce and are only 125 calories each!

Serves: 9

Cooking spray, optional

1 cup (96 g) almond flour

1 tsp coconut flour

½ tsp ground cinnamon

¼ tsp baking soda

1 tbsp (5 g) shredded coconut

2 large eggs

⅓ cup (82 g) unsweetened applesauce

2 tbsp (30 ml) pure maple syrup

1 tsp pure vanilla extract

¼ cup (13 g) shredded carrots

¼ cup (30 g) grated peeled apple

1 tbsp (15 g) coconut oil

Preheat the oven to 375°F (191°C). Prepare a muffin pan with nine muffin liners or spray nine of the cavities with cooking spray.

In a large bowl, mix together the almond flour, coconut flour, cinnamon, baking soda and shredded coconut. In another large bowl, whisk together the eggs, applesauce, maple syrup and vanilla. Fold the flour mixture into the egg mixture. Add the carrots, apple and coconut oil and stir to combine.

Fill the muffin cavities evenly with the batter. Bake the muffins for 22 to 25 minutes, or until a toothpick inserted into the center comes out clean.

Remove the muffins from the oven and let them cool in the muffin pan for 5 minutes before serving.

Store leftover muffins in the refrigerator for up to 7 days or in the freezer for up to 60 days.

Serving Size: ⅑ **Calories:** 125 **Protein:** 4.2 grams **Carbohydrates:** 8 grams **Fiber:** 2.1 grams **Sugar:** 4.6 grams **Fat:** 9.1 grams **Sat. Fat:** 2.1 grams

CALORIES:

165

Serves: 12

LEMON-BLUEBERRY MUFFINS

These lemon-blueberry muffins are fluffy, moist and made with good-for-you ingredients. Made with almond flour and egg whites to increase the protein and fiber content, these muffins will keep you full longer than muffins made with traditional flours. This yummy muffin recipe is a filling grab-and-go snack.

4 large egg whites

1 large egg

¼ cup (60 ml) honey

2 tbsp (30 ml) extra-virgin olive oil

1 tsp pure vanilla extract

2 tbsp (30 ml) fresh lemon juice

2 tsp (4 g) lemon zest

2 cups (192 g) almond flour

½ tsp baking soda

¼ tsp salt

½ cup (50 g) fresh blueberries

Preheat the oven to 350°F (177°C). Line a muffin pan with muffin liners.

In a large bowl, whisk together the egg whites, egg, honey, oil, vanilla, lemon juice and lemon zest until the mixture is bubbly.

In a medium bowl, combine the flour, baking soda and salt. Fold the flour mixture into the egg white mixture until the two are combined. Stir in the blueberries.

Spoon the batter into the muffin cavities until they are three-quarters full, dividing the batter evenly among the cavities. Bake the muffins for 22 to 25 minutes, until a toothpick inserted into the center comes out clean.

Remove the muffins from the oven and let them cool in the muffin pan for 5 minutes before transferring them to a wire baking rack to cool completely.

Store leftover muffins in the refrigerator for up to 7 days or in the freezer for up to 60 days.

Serving Size: ¹⁄₁₂ **Calories:** 165 **Protein:** 5.8 grams **Carbohydrates:** 10.9 grams **Fiber:** 2.8 grams **Sugar:** 7.2 grams **Fat:** 12 grams **Sat. Fat:** 1.1 grams

ACKNOWLEDGMENTS

It's always been a dream of mine to write a cookbook, and I can't believe I just did. In all honesty, I never imagined I would lose weight, change careers, start a website, run a business and write a cookbook all in one lifetime. But I've embraced the fear of what might happen along the way and followed my passion. A huge thank-you to Page Street Publishing for supporting me in that passion!

Thank you to my love, Matt, for being patient and supportive of me during this crazy journey. I couldn't have done it without you testing all of my recipes. Even if they had zucchini, cauliflower and black beans snuck in them—oops!

Thank you to my best friend, Sarah, for telling me I could do this amid a million other things I was juggling in my life. You're always the positive encouragement in my life and the one who pushes me out of my comfort zone.

Thank you to my parents for telling me since I was a child not to follow everyone else and to be different. You gave me the confidence I needed to keep pursuing my dreams. Love you!

Lastly, thank you to my amazing readers and followers for your support throughout the years. I love connecting with you on the blog, as well as through email and social media. Your support and love of my recipes and quirky personality is what brought this cookbook to fruition.

And to the person who purchased this book, a big thank-you! I hope the recipes bring you good health and that my weight-loss story helps you see the opportunity you have to pursue your dreams.

ABOUT THE AUTHOR

Megan Olson is a nutrition practitioner who helps women over thirty-five lose 20 to 50 pounds (9 to 23 kg) or more and keep the weight off for good. She coaches clients one-on-one and in group programs remotely. She's the creator of Skinny Fitalicious, a website with healthy, lightened-up recipes for weight loss.

Megan lost 80 pounds (36 kg) in 2009 by walking and slowly making healthier swaps to her diet. She started Skinny Fitalicious to share healthy, easy recipes that help other women on their weight-loss journeys as well as to share her own health struggles.

Megan is living with Hashimoto's disease and is a cycle instructor. She enjoys fitness, hiking and traveling.

INDEX